MORE QUAKER LAUGHTER

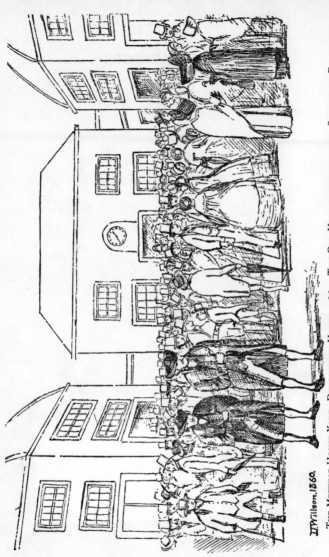

J. Wilson. 1860.

THE MEETING HOUSE YARD, DEVONSHIRE HOUSE, 1860. THE OLD HEADQUARTERS OF THE SOCIETY OF FRIENDS, BUILT IN 1791 AND DEMOLISHED IN 1925.

The two figures in the foreground are exact representations of two ancient Friends (the brothers Bratt) who continued to wear the old Quaker costume of their father's day, and were notable figures at Yearly Meetings.

MORE
QUAKER LAUGHTER

Collected by

WILLIAM H. SESSIONS

WILLIAM SESSIONS LIMITED
YORK, ENGLAND

FIRST PUBLISHED : 1967

SECOND EDITION : 1974

slightly revised

ISBN 0 900657 31 6

Printed in England
in Eric Gill's Perpetua Type
by William Sessions, Limited
The Ebor Press, York

CONTENTS

ILLUSTRATIONS

I am indebted for many of the illustrations to Edward
H. Milligan, Librarian at Friends House, for his kind
research for pictures.

FOREWORD

By 'the son of Quaker Laughter'

The opening sentence of my Father's Introduction which follows was alas, prophetic, for I must in sadness record that William Haughton Sessions, J.P., died on 30th October, 1966, at the fine age of 88 after a full and happy life.

The many sides of his life were amply illustrated during his Memorial Service held in the large Meeting House at Clifford Street, York (the scene of the pair of illustrations on pages 46 and 47), for amongst others, there were vocal contributions from a fellow magistrate, his eldest grandson, a member of The Retreat staff, the British Printing Federation Director, one of his foremen from The Ebor Press, and a director of York City Football Club of which William Sessions was President. Even on that occasion kindly humour shone through the sadness and it seemed wholly fitting for Bootham's Senior Master to include the apocryphal story firmly believed in by many past generations of schoolboys, that if York City had won on the Saturday, William Sessions was likely to minister on the following day at Meeting.

Even within a month or so of his death, my Father was able to gain quiet enjoyment in preparing for publication the words and illustrations for this his posthumous volume, and I vividly recall a little family tea party in a bedroom of my home just two weeks before he died there, when my Father in his easy chair, regaled us with the substance of the York Friends Rowing Club story recounted on page 120.

Kindly humour was indeed ever close to the centre of my Father's being, touching with gold his gentle but steadfast wisdom. As we of the family read and re-read the pages of this his second book of Quaker humour, we can almost hear the quiet chuckle in his voice and see the smile which shines through the printed tale. So my heartfelt wish is that something of my Father's wise humorous philosophy may brush off on you, as you read these pages, like pollen on a bee. If so, you will like us, find your lives enriched and uplifted, enabling us all to continue going forth into the world answering that of God in all men, *cheerfully*.

W.K.S.

INTRODUCTION

'I DO HOPE TO SEE ANOTHER VOLUME BEFORE I DIE', was the kindly message of an American Friend to me. Here was a call with some pathos, and there at my elbow was a card index full of unpublished Quaker stories. The only difficulty was that at 88 I do not rise to a new venture with the same zest as when younger.

I received another urge from America—'It is heart warming to read in *The Friend* that another collection of *Laughter in Quaker Grey*—quaint Quaker Quips and Quotations for the Quizzical—looms up on the horizon. Power to thy right arm, and I do hope it gets into print forthwith.' This was indeed a thrill, as the letter was headed 'Philadelphia Yearly Meeting'. Alas! it was not a Minute of that weighty body, but a private expression of opinion!

Friends in this country, and in countries overseas, have treated my first volume most kindly. I liked one especially who wrote: 'It is quite a relief from the strain of the all too serious-minded Quaker conferences to know there is still much happy Quaker laughter, all part of our Kingdom of God'. To level this up a South African Friend, sending me a new story, added about my first effort, *Laughter in Quaker Grey*. 'Your tale about The Retreat sounds so bad that one suggests with hesitation that perhaps your home should be within those boundaries?' I am glad he ended those remarks with that query mark! However, as I was Treasurer of The Retreat for over 33 years, that Mental Hospital is very near to my heart.

CAPPER'S THE DRAPERS: 1860

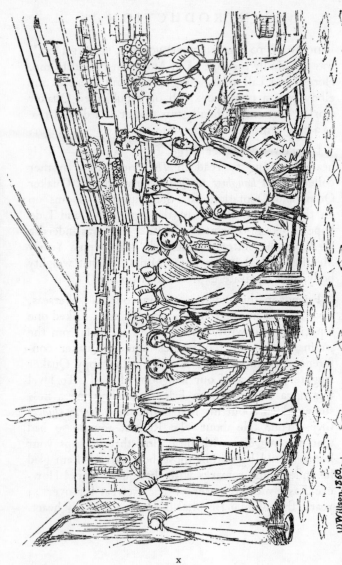

W.Willson. 1860.

It would appear that Friends made other uses of a visit to London than just attending Yearly Meetings.

CHAPTER I

THE QUEST FOR SIMPLICITY

Quaker Dress

Quakerism arose at a time when people's rank was reflected by their dress, so the Quakers chose the dress of the ordinary men and women of that time, as a testimony that all were equal under God, and they kept to this dress in protest against the changing fashions of the world around them.

In later days it did become almost a uniform and one worthy Quakeress was most annoyed when she found her milliner had put an extra tuck in her bonnet, and straightway sent it back to be altered.

The younger Quakeresses were restive about this uniformed dress and were often in trouble with their elders because of attempted improvements.

Thus we get Minutes of Women's Meetings condemning the cutting away of bonnets at the back, so as to show the neck and a little of the hair; Minutes too against pulling out the hair at the front. It was also

Naughty to Show Ears

A Minute of Yorkshire Women's Quarterly Meeting in 1716 runs:—'Though we would not be so particular as to touch upon everything observable in some of our youth who are not so well as we do desire, yet we think it meet to mention to you some things that seem to be growing upon our young

women which are according to the vain fashions of
the world which we could advise against, *viz.*:—
That young Friends dress their hair in a more decent
and modest form that is not to set their headdress
so far back that their ears are part bare, cut and
powdered, frisling out upon their brows also the
strands of their quoif so thin that their ears may
be plainly seen through them.'

Friends' Gowns Made Indecently!

As further evidence of the great difficulty in
keeping the young women to Friends' costume, an
Epistle (1712) of the Yorkshire Women's Meeting,
which is almost entirely occupied with the subject
of dress, concludes 'this hath been recommended
time after time'. It says (*sic*):—

'Many things came under our consideration, and
we desire an alteration in those things that Truth's
testimony is gone out against, which is as follows, *viz.*:
the Friends Gowns made indecently, one part over
long and the other too short, with leade in the sleeves,
and that ffriends should come to a Stability and be
satisfied in the Shape & Compas that Truth leads
into, without changing as the World Changes, allso
Black or coloured Silk or Muslin approns as likewise
hoods or Scarvs not to be over long or broad, and
we desire that friends keepe clear of putting on their
handkerchiefs according to the fashion of the world
leaving their necks bare behind, and allso that Ffriends
cloaths may be of a decent modest colour, not hair
cut or powdered and neither coives to be made with

gathers on the forehead. Bordering on the fashion of the world, those things ffriends Judgement is gone out against.'

(Note the spellings, 'Friends', 'friends' 'Ffriends' and 'ffriends', the first and the last two being possessive).

The difficulty with the 'young things' started early in Quaker history, for even George Fox had to reprove both men and women Friends. Indeed his rebuke is an interesting side-light on the fashions of the second half of the seventeenth century.

George Fox on Dress, 1668

'Away with your skimming-dish hats, and your unnecessary buttons on the top of your sleeves, shoulders, backs, and behind on your coats and cloaks. And away with your long slit yokes on the skirts of your waistcoat; and short sleeves, and pinching your shoulders so as you cannot make use of your arms, and your short black aprons and some have none. And away with your visors, whereby you are not distinguished from bad women, and bare necks, and needless flying scarves like rollers on your back.'

There is a distinction between George Fox on dress and many of the Minutes of Men's and Women's Meetings of a later date. George Fox was advocating simplicity in dress, rather than following the fashions of the day; the later Minutes were trying to keep Friends in a style of dress.

William Charles Braithwaite has put this very clearly:

'It is often assumed that the uniformity of dress which came to prevail among Friends goes back to the early days of the movement; and that Quakerism was born in a plain coat and a broad brimmed hat. But it is evident to the careful student that at first the stress was laid on simplicity rather than uniformity. The Quaker dressed according to his station in life, but without superfluity or ostentation.'

Uniformity has gone, does simplicity remain? Do we dress 'without superfluity or ostentation?' Does it mean that the Quakeress should look 'nice', rather than that the attraction should be her clothes and make up?

Who am I that I should discuss what should be the Quaker or, more difficult, the Quakeress dress to-day? I know it should be simple rather than ostentatious, but I remember some words in a novel, 'she was wearing a dress so beautifully simple that I knew it had come straight from Paris', so I will hasten out of the deep waters of how a Quakeress should dress to-day!

Superfluous Part

That the aim of early Friends was simplicity is well brought out by a Minute or Epistle of Yorkshire Women's Quarterly Meeting of 7th month 1714 held at York which records:

'It is the judgement of friends that we should keep clear from wearing long cloaks and bonnitts to them, and likewise to refrain from having fine tea tables set with fine china, seeing it is more for sight than service, and that friends keep clear of the superfluous part in drinking tea, we thinking that some of the time and money that's spent thus might be made better use of. It's advised that frds should not have so much cheval or earthenware set on their mantel-pieces or on their chests of drawers, but rather sett them in their clositts untill they have occassion to use them, and likewise to keep from using painted calicos.'

In conclusion it is recommended that two women Friends should be chosen in each Preparative Meeting to inspect families and advise or caution them with regard to 'person, habit, or house furniture'.

Having tried my own hand at defining simplicity, I view with much sympathy the task of the 'two women Friends in each Preparative Meeting.'

Dress at Yearly Meeting

When 'marrying out' meant disownment, it was only natural that Yearly and Quarterly Meetings were a gathering ground for younger Friends. It was also natural that young women Friends should endeavour to make themselves as attractive as possible within the limits of the Quaker costume—and just a little bit beyond it! Although some mothers were prepared to turn a blind eye to this 'little bit beyond it', the Women's Meetings were not! The Minutes of one Women's Meeting show that young Friends were directed to appear before it 'in the costumes they intend to wear at Yearly Meeting'. A Minute of the next meeting further records that 'some were directed to make certain alterations, so as to make their appearance more seemly'!

There is much human nature in this blind eye of the mothers who desired to further the hopes of their daughters—but were overruled by the Women's Meetings.

Strings

I remember the neatly tied grey silk ribbons of the Quaker bonnets worn in York in my childhood and it was news to me that at one time they were considered 'worldly' as this Irish story shows:—

Betsy Pike, like other plain Friends of her day, did not wear strings to her bonnet, until attending the Quarterly Meeting at Enniscorthy, where crossing the bridge on a windy day, her bonnet was blown into the river Slaney. After this accident her scruples on the subject of strings were removed!

Two Sorts of Dress

Advice and warning were alike thrown away on some refractory young women in Thirsk Monthly Meeting as the following instance from a Minute on 1797 will show:—

'We are informed that Dorothy Garbutt, a young women of Rounton particular Meeting, hath for a considerable time been very inconsistent particularly in respect to Dress, being accustomed to have two sorts of dress, one to attend Meetings, the other fairs, Markets, etc., for which the Overseers hath had an opportunity with her but she dont think there is any rong in it, and of late there is a matter of greater inconsistency carried to friends Notice on which account she hath also been spoke to, but denyes its being truth, tho' friends from inquiry think there is no doubt thereof, her case is laid before the Men's Meeting, and this meeting appoints (three Friends) to join the men's appointment to pay the said Young Woman a Visit on account thereof.' Next month report is made that 'the said Visit was not to satisfaction', and 'A testemony of Denial' is to be drawn up against her.

Satan and Satin

Rebukes were not always well received and certainly in this case the women got in an effective 'last word'. Nicholas Wain once rebuked a fashionable young lady, with, 'Satin without, and Satan within'. She retorted, 'How can you blame me when old Nick is about'.

The Dying out of Quaker Costume

The use of Quaker costume did not cease by any Minute of the Society, but gradually died out. E. Vipont Brown said that 'In 1872 I went to Bootham School and in Meeting sat facing a long row of broad-brimmed hats and Quaker bonnets. Yet by 1886 the Quaker men's costume had entirely died out, and there were only three Quaker bonnets left, only one being in the Ministers' Gallery'. This quotation of E. Vipont Brown throws some light on the timing of these changes in York meeting.

I was born in 1878 and can remember no York man Friend in Quaker costume. We had the three Quaker bonnets. These passed away with their owners. Then there were none, but up to the turn of the century there was in many Meetings an aged woman Friend still dressing in Quaker costume.

Ear-Rings

There was a very wise remark on the subject of ear-rings. Madeleine Brun (1777-1861) of the famous Brun family who joined Friends in 1788, once asked a weighty English Friend, sojourning in Congenier, if it were really naughty to wear ear-rings. He replied, 'If they are heavy to thee, put them off; if not, keep them'.

When Trousers were Troublesome

It seems strange that the wearing of trousers by men should have been a cause of heart-searching in the Society. They seem so much a part of men's costume to us to-day; but, as this story relates, trousers were troublesome:

When Joseph John Gurney first visited Ireland it was usual for very consistent men Friends to wear the old Quaker costume of knee-breeches. He did not conform in this particular. A concerned Woman Friend expressed the hope that 'J. J. Gurney would see his way out of trousers'.

On the other side of the picture there is a delightful story of modern time about:

Tails

Dr. Henry J. Cadbury learned with dismay that full evening dress, with tails, would be expected at certain evening functions when he went to receive the Nobel Peace Prize. He had no such suit, so he appealed to the Clothing Department of the American Friends Service Committee, who discovered a dress suit just the right size. It was returned after use to be included in the next consignment of clothes for European refugees. It seems a pity that some Friend in 1947 did not offer a suit in exchange, so that these historic tails could be preserved.

It would be interesting to see the refugee in full evening dress walking about his camp, but let us hope it enabled him to get a job as a waiter!

Childish Things

Quakerism must have started about the time when it was the fashion for men to shave. I have no historical data to go upon, but some of the stories which have come down seem to indicate this.

Henry T. Humphries was a young man who wore a beard and moustache. Many plain Friends gave him advice on the subject, among whom was Richard Allen, who counselled him 'to put away childish things!'

On the occasion of Samuel Bewley's wedding at Mountmellick there was a display of fireworks in the Market Square, at which Henry assisted. It was the time of the Crimean War and, seen in the uncertain flashes of light, he was reported to be a Russian. The surprising part of this story to me is that in the Quaker plainness of the 1850's there should be fireworks at a Friends' wedding.

Even a moustache seems to have been frowned upon as witness this story:

The Long Moustache

Friend readers will remember how William Penn was concerned in mind at having to wear a dress sword when attending Court. George Fox comforted him by saying, 'Wear it as long as thou canst'— meaning as long as Penn's conscience would allow him to do it.

Many years afterwards a Friend was reproved for wearing a very long moustache of which he was secretly very proud. He replied that he could justify himself by the words of George Fox himself. He quoted—'Wear it as *long* as thou canst!' putting Fox's words to a very different meaning.

Flowers

Early Quaker simplicity even covered flowers and gardens.

A bowl of flowers is now a regular feature of most Quaker Meetings, so I was interested to read in an account of Henry Newsome that he was 'Very neat and particular about his clothes, he often came to Meeting with a flower in his button hole, but always took it out and left it in the cloakroom before entering Meetings, he said his Mother always did so'.

I am sure flowers would have been thought 'worldly' in an old-time Quaker Meeting, indeed there is a Minute of 1705 on planting gardens that Friends do this 'in a lowly mind, and keep to plainness and the serviceable part'.

In 1956 when I attended Meeting for Sufferings, for the first time, my mind wandered to two things whilst Friends were assembling. First, the bowl of beautiful roses on the Clerk's table, and second, how the present-day members of Sufferings would look in Quaker garb. I had not time to go beyond deciding that the Clerk and the Recording Clerk would have carried the broad-brimmed hat well, and that the Assistant Clerk's face was just made for the Quaker bonnet. Alas! just as I had turned my attention to consider our dear friend Barrow Cadbury in old-time dress, the Meeting started, and I had to turn my thoughts to other matters.

The love of truth in speech, a plain statement, was a feature of Quakerism, which is well illustrated in the following:

Accuracy of Statement

John Woolman's simple accuracy of speech was so well known that two Friends thought they would trap him into an incorrect statement. One Friend called and sat in the parlour with John. The bell was rung by the other Friend—John went to the door, whilst the first Friend slipped out of the window. In answer to the enquiry if his friend were there, John Woolman replied, 'I left him in the parlour'.

The Poley book* gives some cautious statements. Friends in their desire for truth have ever been careful in their statements. Here are a few extreme examples: 'I think or at least I think that I think'. Friend with lumbago 'I have a feeling that is akin to pain'. 'One never knows does one? and when one does one isn't sure, is one?' Quaker, asked about the health of his wife, 'I think I may safely say she is much as she sometimes is'.

It needs the truth to turn to advantage Quaker Customs as will be seen from the story of

Two Drinks

In the course of business a Michelstown, Co. Cork man drove across to a Friend living at Cahir, Co. Tipperary. On the way back the driver said: 'Musha but isnt Mr.——(the Friend) a quare man. He axed me to take a drink I said 'No thank you Sir', and he never axed me a second time. The driver was told in reply that Mr.——was a Friend, and that Quakers have but one word. Shortly afterwards the drive was repeated, and also the invitation to the driver, who promptly replied, 'I will, Sir, two!'

Going One Better

A Quaker in 1677, thought the Friendly plain speech so good that he published a system of plain

Quaker Anecdotes by Ruth and Irwin Poley, published by Pendle Hill.

spelling, *i.e.*, spelling as spoken. He pointed out, *e.g.*, 'righteousness' has four wasted letters and spelt it 'ryteosnes'. Unfortunately Quakers did not add simple spelling to plain speech.

This simplicity went in all details of life, as is seen in

An Irish Retort

An English Friend thought the Irish practice of taking butter with bread and cheese was extravagant; an Irish Friend replied that on the contrary it was economical, for one piece of bread did for both butter and cheese.

Tea Drinking

Quakers in the past looked with disfavour on sugar because it was then the product of slave labour, but it was news to me to learn from the *Friends Historical Journal* of Spring 1961, that some Friends had objected to tea drinking.

Indeed in the 'General Advices in Rhyme' given in *Laughter in Quaker Grey*, tea seems to have special recommendation:

'All places of diversion shun,
Except the tea and modest bun'.

Yet, in 1724, Cork Men's Meeting passed a testimony against tea drinking. It is with very real regret that I am unable to record that Cork Women's Meeting retaliated by passing a testimony against men Friends' smoking!

A more exciting demonstration against the evils of tea drinking was that of Benjamin Lay in 1742. Finding his late wife had a store of china and other tea, he put it all in a case and mounted a stall in

Benjamin Lay.

Philadelphia market. Then with a hammer he proceeded to smash the case, so as to scatter the tea. Bystanders offered to buy it from him, but he refused, and went on with his hammering. At this there was such a rush of people to secure as much as they could of the precious tea, that the stall, Benjamin Lay, and the case of tea were all upset in the scramble. From his portrait opposite he looks eccentric enough for any exploit.

Scandal

Whilst I am for the moment serious! may I introduce two ancient Minutes, because they are needed as much to-day as when they were written. The first is dated 1693:

'If any Friend shall hear a scandalous report concerning any other Friend, it is thought convenient and christian like, that such do forthwith acquaint the party concerned of the said report, and not tell it to others, or spread it abroad whisperingly.'

The second is dated 1719:

'If you hear a report of a Friend (to his disadvantage) be careful not to report it again, but go to the person of whom the report is, and enquire if it be true, or not; and if it be true, then deal with such a person for it, according to the doctrine of Christ, in Matth. xviii 16, 17; but if false, then endeavour, as much as in you lies, to stop such report; for, as Solomon says, "A good name is rather to be chosen than great riches".'

Still in serious mood, I do not think the ideal behind the following has ever been put better than it was by Joseph Sturge:—

'The belief that we are responsible for the means of acquiring, as well as for the use we make of our property, and that we cannot exercise too rigid a watchfulness over our *own* conduct, is compatible with perfect charity towards those who differ from us in opinion.'

Real Equality

It is remarkable that centuries before there were any campaigns for Women's Rights, Quakerism gave real equality to men and women.

An outstanding example of this equality was a decision of Yearly Meeting on the subject of women smoking. It was taken in 1919 when women had just started to smoke, and when this was looked upon, even by 'the man in the street', as something 'fast' and daring. Yearly Meeting was deeply concerned that women Friends should not smoke, but it felt that smoking amongst men Friends was so deeply rooted that it could not pass a Minute against all smoking—men and women alike—so it refused to pass a Minute condemning smoking by women.

Smuggled Goods

Friends queries were ever practical; here is an old one:

'Do you stand clear in our Testimony against defrauding the King of his Customs Duties & Excise, or in Dealing in Goods suspected to be Run?'

The last part was an easy one to answer in most Meetings, except in parts of Cornwall, then the home of smuggling, where so many things in the shops could be—'Suspected to be Run'!

Months and Days

The reason for Friends refusing to use the accepted names of the months and days can be seen from the following Minute of London Yearly Meeting in 1697:-

'That all Friends keep to the simplicity of truth, and our ancient testimony, in calling the months and days by scripture and not by heathen.'

Changes in the Calendar

The following extracts from a Minute of The Meeting for Sufferings in London, dated the sixth day of the Seventh Month, 1751, and sent to the Quarterly and Monthly Meetings of Friends in Great Britain, Ireland and America are an interesting record of the change in the calendar ordered by Parliament at this time.

'In all the records and writings of Friends, from and after the last day of the Tenth Month, called December, next, the computation of time established by the said act, should be observed: and that accordingly the first day of the Eleventh Month, commonly called January, next, shall be reckoned and deemed, by Friends, the first day of the First Month of the year 1752.

And whereas for the more regular computation of time, the same Act of Parliament doth direct, that the natural day next immediately following the 'second day of September in the year 1752', shall be called, reckoned, and accounted to be the fourteenth day of September, omitting for that time only the eleven intermediate days of the common calendar!—that Friends should be found in the observance of this direction, and omit the said eleven nominal days accordingly.

And we think it may be useful and expedient, on the present occasion, to revive in your remembrance some of the motives which induced our ancient Friends to forbear the vulgar appellations of the months and days, and to observe in their conversations and writings such names as were agreeable to scripture and the practice of good men therein recorded.

And that you may the more clearly discern the importance of that Christian testimony borne by our predecessors in this case, we recommend what follows to your serious consideration.

A brief account of the origin of the names of some months of the year, and of all the days of the week, now customarily and commonly used.

I.   January was so called from Janus, an ancient King of Italy, whom heathenish superstition had defied, to whom a temple was built, and this month dedicated.

II.   February was so called from Februa, a word denoting purgation by sacrifices; it being useful in this month for the priests of the heathen god Pan to offer sacrifices, to the cleansing or purgation of the people.

III.   March was so denominated from Mars, feigned to be the god of war, whom Romulus, founder of the Roman empire, pretended to be his father.

IV   April is generally supposed to derive its name from the Greek appellation of Venus, an imaginary goddess worshipped by the Romans.

V   May is said to have been so called from Maia the Mother of Mercury, another of their pretended ethnic deities, to whom in this month they paid their devotions.

VI   June is said to take its name from Juno, one of the supposed goddesses of the heathen.

VII   July, so called from Julius Caesar, one of the Roman emperors, who gave his name to this month, which before was called Quintilis, or the Fifth.

VIII   August, so named in honour of Augustus Caesar, another of the Roman emperors. This month was before called Sextilis, or the Sixth.

The other four months, namely, September, October, November, and December, still retain their numerical Latin names; which, according to the late regulation of the calendar, will for the future be improperly applied.

As the idolatrous Romans thus gave names to several of the months in honour of their pretended deities, so the like idolatry prevailing among our Saxon ancestors, induced them to call the days of the week by the name of an idol, which on that day they particularly worshipped, hence:

The first day of the week was by them called Sunday, from their customary adoration of the Sun upon that day.

The second day of the week they called Monday, from their usual custom of worshipping the Moon on that day.

IDOLS OF THE ANCIENT BRITONS AND SAXONS.

SUN MOON TUISCO WODEN THOR FRIGA SEATER

The third day of the week they named Tuesday, in honour of one of their idols called Tuisco.

The fourth day of the week was called Wednesday, from the apellation of Woden, another of their idols.

The fifth day of the week was called Thursday, from the name of an idol called Thor, to whom they paid their devotions upon that day.

The sixth day of the week was termed Friday, from the name of Friga, an imaginary goddess by them worshipped.

The seventh day they styled Saturday, as is supposed from Saturn, or Seater, by them then worshipped.

The popish sacrifice of the mass gave rise to the vulgar names of Michaelmas, Martinmas, Christmas, and the like.

Seeing therefore that these appellations and names of days, months, and times, are of an idolatrous or superstitious original, . . . let not the reproach of singularity . . . discourage you from keeping to the language of truth, in denominating the months and days according to the plain and scriptural way of expression.'

Days of the Week

An *Annual Monitor** backed up its plea for the use of numbers for days and months with the somewhat lurid picture shown opposite of the gods after whom the days of the week were called. It is not a flattering picture, in fact, as drawn, I suggest they look like a bunch of crooks!

*The annual Quaker publication originated by William and Ann Alexander of York in 1813 giving obituary notices and testimonials of Friends who had recently died.

In All Things Charity

I like the story of a woman Friend who complained to an Elder about a Friend attending the Theatre, adding, 'I have never been within the doors of a play-house'. To which the Elder replied, 'Neither have I, but I doubt not many better people have'.

A Jew's Harp

Some will remember in their young days a simple musical instrument, played with the mouth, called a Jew's harp. Prof. Enock, a welcome lecturer in my school days on the trap-door spider and other subjects of natural history, once related how, in his school days at Ackworth, he had been punished for playing a Jew's Harp and the instrument confiscated. This made little noise; his chief offence was the introduction of a musical instrument into a Quaker School.

By the by, Enock was showing us some magnified pictures of minute live insects in drops of water. By mischance two 'enemies' were in one drop of water and started to fight. As they went round and round the screen, the 'Old Adam' overcame Quaker peace principles, and we started to cheer the fight. We never saw which won—the slide was hastily withdrawn!

Music

The early Quaker outlook on music may seem strange to-day, but it had definite foundations. Hymns were not sung in Meeting for Worship, because, in the interest of sincerity and truth, people might be singing something which they did not really feel. I suppose there is something in this outlook. I remember, long ago, seeing a cheerful laddie singing with gusto an old hymn about 'I should like to die and be in heaven'. The contrast between the boy, so full of life, and the words struck me as so terrible that I deliberately made a 'face' at him to make him laugh and forget the words. It was very naughty of me, but I suppose it was the old Quaker outlook on hymns coming out in me.

Secular music was undoubtedly frowned upon by early Quakers because it was associated with 'idle frivolity'.

Musical Festival

There was a Musical Festival in York in 1823. The Minster was used for sacred works, concert halls for secular ones. There were also two balls, including a fancy dress one. James Backhouse published a four-page 'address' against this. The tenor of his remarks may be gathered from the following extracts:

'The Musical Festival is looked upon by some persons as connected with Divine Worship, and by others as a mere piece of amusement. . . . And can anyone suppose that the persons employed to produce this wonderful effect on the imaginations of their hearers, who are selected from Theatres and other places of vain amusement, can be on this occasion transformed into acceptable ministers in the service of Jesus Christ, however sublimely they may sing of his birth, life, death, resurrection, and ascension.'

Whether in these days we agree with him or not, the old Quaker outlook is moderately stated, and James Backhouse makes his point well.

LOVES YOUNG DREAM

CHAPTER II

COURTSHIP AND MARRIAGE

Loves Young Dream

The illustration 'Loves Young Dream' is from the *Darlington Book, and the wording under it is:—

> This is Silas Smith declaring himself before the object of his admiration: being a prudent young man his tactics were characterized by much caution, he did not cast himself upon his knees in a paroxysm of hope and fear. Oh no! that would have been rash, calculated both to injure his trousers and to commit him; he therefore spread his red cotton pocket-handkerchief on the path-way, and kneeling down, observed 'dost thou think a way might open for us to revolve on a mutual Axletree, Deborah Pumphrey?', to which she replied, 'I think I might get to like thee, Silas Smith, if thou would abstain from snuffling in Meeting.'

What an ordeal it must have been in times past for the young folks wishing to marry, to have to appear before three Meetings—the Women's Meeting, the Men's Meeting and a Joint Meeting to state their intentions, and to be examined about 'being clear of all others'.

Clear of all Others

Can we imagine a good Friend getting up and saying, 'William when thou wast at Old Scholars,

*A light-hearted pictorial description of a Friends' First Day Schools' Conference held in Darlington in 1874 (see also page 58).

did I not see thee much engaged with a flaxon-haired girl. Now, William, what about that blonde? Fortunately William has a good answer, for she was married a year ago, but Elizabeth duly notes the blonde as a subject of further enquiry from William!

Elizabeth is not so happy about the next question. 'Elizabeth when didst thou last hear from James, with whom thou seemed on very friendly terms at Quarterly Meeting a year ago?' Elizabeth's young brother sniggers, for he knows there had been correspondence between the two. She has told William about James, but Elizabeth is a kindly soul. How shall she clear herself before the Meeting, and yet not hurt James's feelings?

Uncontrollable

Thomas N. Cole and Elizabeth Leadbeater were presenting their marriage before one of the three Meetings required. When asked the formal question as to whether they had the consent of their parents to the proposed union, Thomas stood up and said, 'We are uncontrollable!' meaning they had both lost their parents.

Marrying Out

It is well known that a Friend marrying someone not in membership was disowned for 'marrying out'. What is not so well known is that in at least one or two cases the Mother was also disowned, for having 'countenanced her daughter's marrying out'.

Divided but Kindly Counsel

Two Friends were appointed to visit a young woman Friend who contemplated 'marrying out', in the days when this meant disownment. They reasoned with her, but she refused to reconsider her decision. They left her weeping, but one visitor turned back to say, 'Don't cry, lass, if thee wants the man, *have* him!'

The Cow with the Nice Face

I had attended his simple Quaker funeral service, and after it the widow's brother told me how she had met her husband. The family fortunes were not too flourishing, and she, enthusiastic and impetuous, would help. She tried keeping poultry, without much success, and thought milk would pay better. Thus, when a small legacy came from an Aunt, she remembered it was market day in the nearby city, caught the next train, and proceeded to inspect the cows on sale.

Said she to a young farmer, 'I like that cow's face—is it a good cow?' The amused farmer replied, 'perhaps I am not the one you should consult, for I'm selling it, but, as a matter of fact, it is a good cow'. 'I'll buy it', she said, and produced her cheque. The cheque was less than the price the farmer was expecting for the cow, but when she said it was all she had, he let it go. She was staggered at the next remark, 'How are you getting it home?' 'Oh' said she, in dismay, 'I never thought of that!' At which the farmer said he would bring it himself.

Left to her own thoughts in the train home, she realized she liked the face of the young farmer almost as much as that of the cow, so she looked forward with pleasure to seeing the two faces again.

The cow arrived and the farmer enquired, 'Where is the cowhouse?' 'Oh', she said, 'I never thought of that'. However, they found a suitable place in the outbuildings. The young farmer, perhaps because he saw her inexperience, and perhaps because he liked her face even more than she did that of the cow, offered to give her any advice and help she needed. It proved a troublesome cow. Advice seemed always to be needed. In fact his old housekeeper said, with a chuckle, she always knew there was trouble with that cow when the master knocked off work a bit earlier, and went off in his best suit. So the sight of a cow with a nice face resulted in two delightful Friends having a happy married life together.

I wonder what the young men of the Meeting thought of the appearance of a stranger in

Scarlet and Velvet

At the very beginning of the eighteenth century, Reuben Fisher came to visit her sister Martha, who was living in Ireland, at Youghal, and had become a Friend. He was then described as a gay young man in scarlet, with velvet breeches. He attended Church in the morning, but later in the day came to Friends' Meeting. He must have caused some fluttering of the heart amongst the young women, with his London manners, and his scarlet and velvet standing out from the greys and drabs of the rest of the company. We can speculate too whether that first attendance at Friends' Meeting was to please his sister or because of Margaret Shute, whom he afterwards married!

Here is another Irish story:

The Spark of Beauty

A young Friend was explaining to a group of young men, not all Quakers, the accomplishments he would require in the girl he married. One of his companions exclaimed, 'Ah, Will, it would take a very spark of beauty to please you!' The phrase stuck and, when he married, Will's wife was known in Limerick as 'the spark of beauty', an unusually frivolous description for a woman Friend in Quaker costume.

Consent of Parents

Samuel Grubb came to ask for Margaret Shackleton. Her Father, Richard Shackleton, and his wife Elizabeth, were considering his proposal. Elizabeth Shackleton objected because he had buttons on the back of his coat, condemned by strict Quakers as a most fashionable adornment. Richard Shackleton observed, 'If he's right to a button, my dear, he will do'.

Dale Courtship

The simple life of the north-country dales of necessity bred simple character. In the old farmhouse of Sykelands, under Rysell, dwelt Thomas Sedgwick, but all the Dale called him, 'Tammas O' Sykelands', and his house was kept by a young woman Friend,

Margaret Hayton. Thomas had turned his fortieth year, and no one thought he would ever marry, but this is what passed between him and his housekeeper one May morning, when Margaret was in the yard, feeding the calves. Thomas had been wandering aimlessly about for ten minutes, and was now at the gate.

'Margaret?' 'Yes, Tammas'. 'How auld may thou be?' 'Comin' twenty-three, Tammas!' 'Eh, I nivver thout tha was as young, but mebbe thou'll mend o' that?' 'Sure, Tammas'. A prolonged pause followed, during which Margaret was busier at her work than ever. Then Thomas began again, 'Margaret?' 'Eh.' 'Thou be'est ower young, Marget'. A pause, then, 'I'd just a thowt that if iverr I sud marry, it ud ha' been a like bunchy lass sic as thee, but'; then another pause, 'Dost though really think thou'ld mend Marget?' 'Eh, no-one ivver asked me that question afore, Tammas'. 'Well, Marget, Ise' goin' into Garsdale for t'week-end. When I come back if thou'rt of t'same mind, I dunno but what it 'ud be reet that we s'ud wed Marget. I allus thowt I mun has' a like bunchy body. Eh, Marget'. 'Yes, Tammas'.

When the next Monthly Meeting took place Thomas was congratulated on having obtained as his wife such a good housekeeper, and such a quiet-spoken woman, as was Margaret Hayton.

This next story was sent to me from New Zealand:

The Gypsy Fortune Teller

'The pretty Miss Richards', as she was known in Redruth, was walking in the town in Quaker dress, when a gypsy woman tried to stop her, to tell her fortune. Not approving she passed on, and the woman called after her, 'I'll tell 'ee just the same, your future husband is on the next coach, so look out!' A young Friend was on the next coach; later when she was going to visit an aunt, he stole up to her and whispered, 'Don't thee get engaged whilst thou'st away', and later still married her. The question is, was this accurate gypsy fortune telling, or did the gypsy work on the mind of the maiden?

A Tale of a Coat Tail

William Boake was deeply attached to Euphemia Birkett, but her aunt and guardian, Catherine Tew, did not desire the match. On the occasion of his call she arranged that Euphemia should be in an upper room. William Boake, who was of an ardent and impetuous nature, was not to be put off in this manner, so ran up the stairs, Catherine Tew following. She caught hold of the tail of his coat, which gave way, and remained in her hand.

William Boake kept on his course, won his lady-love, and they were later married. He preserved the one-tail coat for many years as a memento.

Elopement from Yearly Meeting

A Quakeress from Norfolk eloped from Yearly Meeting in a public coach to meet her future husband, who was an actor. She got rid of her Friends' bonnet by crushing it under the seat of the coach.

Careful Accuracy?

A Quaker, hesitating whether or not to propose over tea in the girl's home, was asked if he would have another cup. He said, 'half-a-cup please', and the cup came back exactly half-full. This careful accuracy so pleased him that he proposed, and was accepted.

Some years afterwards, the matter of his proposal came up, and he told his wife what had decided him. 'Oh', said his wife, 'I remember that afternoon well, there wasn't another drop in the teapot'.

Wild Oats

Mother to her non-Friend son, whom she suspected of falling in love with a Quakeress. 'You know you'll have to sow your wild oats quickly, if you are attracted in that quarter.' Son, 'It's all right, Mother, I'm only going to sow my Quaker Oats!'

Saying the Words

Saying the words which unite them at a Quaker wedding is always an ordeal to the bride and bridegroom. The occasion is a solemn one, momentous in its effect on life, and however well the words have been learned beforehand, there is the nervous tension of the moment to overcome. Little wonder that mistakes sometimes occur as is illustrated in the following story:

The bridegroom was saying his words clearly and well, but accidentally introduced some 'embroidery' into the concluding sentence, which considerably startled his bride. The bridegroom finished with, 'Until it shall please the Lord, in his infinite mercy, by death to separate us.'*

Those who take part in the service are almost always helpful and in full sympathy with the occasion, but very, very rarely other thoughts intrude, or the speakers do not use 'well chosen words'.

Wedding Text

At a Quaker wedding, a woman Minister rose in the silence, and said, 'Are not two sparrows sold for a farthing?' and sat down. The feelings of the bride and bridegroom are not recorded.

Sermon at a Wedding Service

A. Ward Applegate tells in *The American Friend* the story of a woman who was apt to speak too often in the ministry. It was delicately suggested to her by two Friends that she should be silent during a Quaker wedding which was about to begin. All through the morning worship she brooded over the fact that she had been thus 'disciplined' by her two well-meaning Friends. It proved to be too great a burden for her

---

* Friends are not married by any Minister or Elder, but the couple stand up in a Meeting for Worship and make the following declaration—'Friends, I take this my friend ———— to be my wife, promising through Divine assistance to be unto her a loving and faithful husband, until it shall please the Lord by death to separate us.' The woman follows with the same declaration, suitably altered.

spirit to bear. Consequently, in the weighty silence which immediately preceded the marriage ceremony, and while the hearts of the young couple thumped in their bosoms as they made ready to stand together and say their vows, this Friend, having in mind only those who had privately disciplined her, nothing more, arose and in a clear, shrill voice, quoted simply—'Father, forgive them, for they know not what they do'.

These Young People

The desire of Quakers to be strictly accurate was illustrated at a marriage service between a bridegroom of 32 and a bride of 29.

During the meeting a woman Friend prayed, 'for a blessing on these two young', then she paused, and went on, 'these moderately young people'.

Cheers in Meeting

There was an unusual ending to the wedding of Arnold S. Rowntree and May Harvey. Arnold was a well-loved Adult School teacher, and a number of his class went from York to Leeds for the wedding. At the end of Meeting, when the bridal couple rose to leave, they gave them three hearty cheers to show their affection.

Enjoyment in Ireland

Who would have thought of this 'going-on' at an old-time Quaker Wedding? Let me add, in case it is thought some humorist has been 'pulling my leg', the story is told by Isabel Grubb.

Irish Young Friends seem to have enjoyed themselves thoroughly at weddings, for we find Quaker Business Meetings protesting against 'the heathenish custom' of pulling off the bride's garter, and throwing her stocking. The direction in which the stocking fell was supposed to show the person who was to be married next!

Crown for a Wife

A Quaker married a woman of the Church of England, and the vicar asked a crown for his fee. Money was much more valuable then, and the Quaker thought the fee high, but he said he would pay if the clergyman could show him a text of Scripture proving his fees were a crown. The vicar quoted—'A virtuous woman is a crown to her husband'. The Quaker paid.

Present Wife

Overheard at a Yorkshire Quarterly Meeting: Woman Friend to another, who was the third wife of a well-known Quaker, 'Oh thou'rt ———'s wife, art thou? Art thou his present wife?'

Elizabeth Fry

An Irish Friend was walking in an English garden in company with Elizabeth Fry and her husband. Elizabeth Fry had her hand on the arm of her husband, who caressingly stroked it, and asked, 'Samuel, did'st thou admire my wife's hand in Ireland?' Samuel with true Irish gallantry replied, 'We saw so much to admire, that we did not descend to particulars'.

Grandmothers

A Friend, the morning after his first child was born, met William Tallack, and told him of the fact, and said the child's name was 'Phoebe'. 'Oh', said William Tallack, 'isn't that rather an old grandmotherly name?' 'Yes', said the father, 'but I suppose they must begin as babies'. William replied, 'Well, I never thought of that!'

Indiscreet Friend

Elizabeth Shackleton once, under some provocation, said to her husband, 'Thou art an indiscreet, elderly Friend'. He replied, 'My heart, another would have said I was an old fool'.

The World is Queer

Quaker husband to wife—'All the world is queer except thee and me, and even thee's a little queer sometimes'.

Yorkshire Quakers

Me dowter worked for Quaker folk, a reet funny lot. When she went into t'parlour, they'd all be sat wi their 'eeds i their 'ands, and niver speak a word, but t'lass just went on wi' 'er work. When she axed 'em what for they kept so quiet, t'Missus sed they nobbut speak when t'spirit moves 'em. My dowter says of 'er young man, 'Yon Sam's a nice chap, but 'es like a Quaker, 'e's a funny un. Sometimes 'e'll ee yer, sometimes not; 'appen if t'spirit moves 'im 'e offer'.

I will finish this chapter with a story of long ago, of how two people had to be married three times before everyone was satisfied.

Triple Tie Rewritten

A widowed Friend in the north had an ailing daughter, and found a girl from a neighbouring family to be her companion. Gossip came to the mother's ears that this girl was 'setting her cap' at her only son, and she was much upset. An outraged father came to take his daughter home, but the girl hid in a loft, having first met the young man, who quietly told her to meet him at a certain gate that evening. Later he saddled two horses, and, leaving one of his coat tails in his protesting mother's hands, rode up to the gate with a groom. They met the waiting girl and set off for Gretna Green, she, out of respect for the proprieties riding behind the groom.

After the marriage next morning it was seemly that husband and wife should ride together so the groom was sent home to break the news. The couple came back by longer and pleasanter ways to face the disapproval of both parents.

Friends disowned them, but the local minister insisted that he be allowed to marry them in church to satisfy the bride's father. Family tradition tells that eventually they were also married in Meeting. It is certain that the bride soon applied for membership, and that they were joyfully taken back into the Society.

The foregoing is an amendment to the 'Triple Tie' story which appeared on pages 37-38 of the first edition of *More Quaker Laughter*. This corrected version has kindly been sent by Hannah Taylor, eldest daughter of William Cadbury and co-author of *Traveller's Joy*.

The bridegroom in the elopement story, which took place in 1824, was Isaac Hall (1793-1861) who farmed High Studden, two miles outside Allendale in Northumberland. The bride was Mary Philipson (1807-1853) daughter of Frank Philipson, a small tenant farmer and lead miner. Of their 10 children, the eldest was called, Hannah, after whom Hannah Taylor is named, being a great-grand-daughter on the distaff side. The helpful clergyman in the story charged no fee for marrying them.

CHAPTER III

HUMOUR AT MEETINGS

Still-born Silence

There are few passages by non-Friends about the Quaker Meeting which can compare with Charles Lamb's description in his *Essays of Elia*.

'Still-born Silence! thou that art
Flood-gate of the deeper heart!
Offspring of a heavenly kind!
Frost o' the mouth, and thaw o' the mind!
Secrecy's confident, and he
Who makes religion mystery!
Admiration's speaking'st tongue!
Leave, thy desert shades among,
Reverend hermits' hallow'd cells,
Where retired devotion dwells!
With thy enthusiasms come,
Seize our tongues, and strike us dumb!

READER, would'st thou know what true peace and quiet mean; would'st thou find a refuge from the noises and clamours of the multitude; would'st thou enjoy at once solitude and society; would'st thou possess the depth of thine own spirit in stillness, without being shut out from the consolatory faces of thy species; would'st thou be alone and yet accompanied; solitary, yet not desolate; singular, yet not without some to keep thee in countenance; a unit in aggregate; a simple in composite:—come with me into a Quakers' Meeting.

THE WOMEN'S SIDE. YEARLY MEETING, 1860

J.Willson. 1860.

H.W.Willson. 1860.

THE MEN'S SIDE, YEARLY MEETING, 1860

41

Dost thou love silence deep as that 'before the winds were made?' go not out into the wilderness, descend not into the profundities of the earth; shut not up thy casements; nor pour wax into the little cells of thy ears, with little-faith'd self-mistrusting Ulysses.—Retire with me into a Quakers' Meeting.

For a man to refrain even from good words, and to hold his peace, it is commendable: but for a multitude, it is a great mystery.

What is the stillness of the desert, compared with this place? Silence her sacred self is multiplied and rendered more intense by numbers, and by sympathy. She too hath her deeps, that call into deeps. Negation itself hath a positive more or less; and closed eyes would seem to obscure the great obscurity of midnight.

They are wounds, which an imperfect solitude cannot heal. By imperfect I mean that which a man enjoyeth by himself. The perfect is that which he can sometimes attain in crowds, but nowhere so absolutely as in a Quakers' Meeting.

The Abbey Church of Westminster hath nothing so solemn, so spirit-soothing, as the naked walls and benches of Quakers' Meeting. O when the spirit is sore fettered, even tired to sickness of the janglings, and nonsense-noises of the world, what a balm and a solace it is, to go and seat yourself for a quiet half hour, upon some undisputed corner of a bench, among the gentle Quakers!

Their garb and stillness conjoined, present a uniformity, tranquil and herd-like—as in the pasture —'forty feeding like one.'—

The very garments of a Quaker seem incapable of receiving a soil; and cleanliness in them to be something more than the absence of its contrary. Every Quakeress is a lily; and when they come up in bands to their Whitsun-Conferences, whitening the easterly steets of the metropolis, from all parts of the United Kingdom, they show like troops of the Shining Ones'.

Eating as a Horse

Thinking of the old-time Quaker has made me wonder if we have changed our ways of eating, as well as dress and other things.

Listen to Charles Lamb again in his chapter 'Grace before meat'. 'The Quakers who go about their business, of every description, with more calmness than we, have more title to the use of these benedictory prefaces.

I have always admired their silent grace, and the more because I have observed their applications to the meat and drink following to be less passionate and sensual than ours. They are neither gluttons nor winebibbers as people. They eat, as a horse bolts his chopt hay, with indifference, calmness and cleanly circumstances. They neither grease nor slop themselves.'

What a delightful Query it would be for any Yearly Meeting to send down—'Do Friends when eating neither grease or slop themselves, but rather eat as a horse bolts his chopt hay! ! '

We thank thee Charles Lamb.

Difficulty of Persecutors

One difficulty in persecuting Quakers was that a Meeting required no outward implements, and worshipped equally well in silence as in speech.

A Quaker Meeting just gathers.

Professor David Manson puts this well:

'You may break in upon them, hoot at them, war at them, drag them about; the meeting, if it is of any size, still goes on till all the component individuals are murdered. Throw them out of the doors in twos and threes, and they but re-enter at the window and quietly resume their places. Pull their meeting-house down, and they re-assemble next day most punctually amidst the broken walls and rafters. Shovel sand or earth down upon them, and there they sit, a sight to see, musing, immovable among the rubbish.'

People or Buildings

An American taxi driver of Italian origin had to transport some Friends Relief goods from one Meeting House to another. He looked round with interest, noted the absence of altar, crucifix, and stained glass, and said, 'These Quakers spend money for people, instead of buildings'.

Sword and Mace in York Meeting

I saw these illustrations about seventy-three years ago, and was not present at the Meeting, as I was away at School, and so perhaps can be pardoned for not getting the details correct in *Laughter in Quaker Grey*, but now I have secured reproductions of the actual pictures.

'On Sunday last, a rather unusual ceremony took place at the Friends' Meeting House, when the Lord Mayor (Mr. Alderman Clayton), who is a member of the Society of Friends, attended the service in state. He was accompanied by the City Sheriff, Aldermen, and members of the Corporation, all wearing their official robes; a stand had previously been put up to receive the sword and mace, not, however, without some scruples on the part of a number of the "Friends" as to the propriety of admitting the insignia.'

The Friends in the Ministers Gallery are:
Left to right: A. Neave Brayshaw, J. Wilhelm Rowntree, John Firth Fryer, John Stephenson Rowntree, Fielden Thorp, Elizabeth G. Dimsdale and Mary Sessions (the author's mother).

The first three below are:
Left to right: the Town Clerk, The Lord Mayor and the Sheriff.

In the haste of sketching the artist has left the ends of the sword and the mace unsupported, he has put the Sheriff's chain on the Lord Mayor, and left the Sheriff without one, and put a queer Quaker bonnet on Mary Sessions, who did not wear one, although Elizabeth G. Dimsdale did.

THE SWORD AND MACE IN YORK MEETING—*from the 'Daily Graphic'*

THE SWORD AND MACE IN YORK MEETING—*as seen by 'Punch'*

The *Punch* wording was as follows:—

Decidedly Quaint

'What must have been an interesting ceremony took place at the Friends' Meeting House, York, when the Lord Mayor, who is a member of the Society of Friends, attended the service in state, on which occasion, as appears from a picture in the *Daily Graphic* of April 13, somebody chucked the sword of state on to the head of His Worship sitting below, while somebody else in turn-down collars most unwarrantably whacked the bald skull of a peaceable old gentleman with the official mace! ! Some of the excellent Friends must have been inclined to raise a protest against the dramatic action of Punch and Judy being introduced within the walls of a decorous meeting house. Their scruples, we may suppose, were ultimately satisfied.'

Reproduced by permission of 'Punch'

A glance at the *Daily Graphic* picture will show how easy it was for the *Punch* artist to suggest from it an uproarious scene, instead of a Meeting at prayer (which fact he would not know).

J. Wilhelm Rowntree is bringing the mace down on his Uncle's head, whilst apparently A. Neave Brayshaw is flinging the sword to alight crack on the Lord Mayor's head. Even more amazing (or humorous) the gas lamp has been taken off its pipe and becomes a glass of brandy in Fielden Thorp's hand, and his face is touched up to give him a suggestion of enjoying glasses of brandy. Fielden Thorp, retired Head of Bootham, was a staunch teetotaller, who wore a bit of blue ribbon on his coat, as was the custom then, to show publicly that he was an abstainer.

Simplicity

Rufus Jones once attended a Friends' Summer School at Kirkbymoorside. He gave several learned and most interesting lectures. On Sunday evening he was asked to preach at the Methodist Chapel. Many from outlying Dales attended and the Chapel was packed. I wondered how so learned a man would be able to appeal to the simpler country folk. To my surprise he gave a wonderful sermon, with a direct appeal to his audience. He was clear and simple both in matter and in the words used. His learned gifts were there, but they were clothed in sweet simplicity.

Long years afterwards I heard a story which Rufus Jones said had been a great lesson to him. It was a lesson he had certainly already learnt when he preached that sermon at Kirkbymoorside. The story is: Rufus Jones had spoken in a country Meeting. His learned discourse was well above the heads of the Company. After he sat down a woman Friend rose, and said, 'Christ said, "Feed my sheep, not feed my giraffes" ', and sat down.

Silent Meeting

A mother had taken her small son to Meeting for the first time, and after they had been sitting for a little time without anything being said, the little chap asked in an audible voice. 'Mother, why are they all sitting so silently?' The mother hushed the child. Shortly afterwards a Friend rose, and began, 'Our first speaker this morning has put before us a most important question'.

Reading the Bible

I know that reading from notes was not allowed by early Clerks in Yearly Meeting. I have come across one example of objection to reading the Bible in Meeting, but I do not think this was general.

Asses Twain

A woman Friend felt so strongly that a case of discipline had been settled in a way of which she did not approve that she conceived it her duty to preach on all occasions from the text, 'The innocent suffer, while the guilty go free'. Friends continually remonstrated with her, but to no avail, until positive action became necessary. When next she rose and commenced her usual address, women elders gave the signal, and two lusty men Friends walked gravely to her side, and cautioned her to desist, upon penalty of removal if she refused. She took no notice of them, but continued her sermon. Whereupon they quickly picked her up, and bore her down the aisle to the door. During her progress she startled the congregation by exclaiming, 'I am more honoured than our Lord. He was carried on the back of one ass, while I am borne on the backs of two'.

Quotations

Fielden Thorp, a former Head of Bootham, and for many years head of York Meeting, had a wonderful memory for quotations. Many a speaker, starting a quotation, and then stumbling over it, was prompted by Fielden. Once, however, a speaker said he would like to quote some lines from Frances Ridley Havergill, then stopped. He looked appealingly at Fielden Thorp, but even that oracle could not prompt a quotation which had not begun.

Any Work

In the Second World War, Cirencester Meeting House was lent to the Ministry of National Insurance on condition that the Committee Room was retained, together with the right to use the large Meeting Room occasionally, without disturbing National Insurance fixtures.

Thus it was that at one Meeting, Friends gathered in silence, faced with a large notice, 'If you have done ANY work since you last attended, you must say so immediately!'

Awake thou that Sleepeth!

A Friend wrote: 'I thought of your book during last Monthly Meeting, when the following incident occurred, and as Clerk, I had to try to keep a reasonably straight face:—

In the silence of the Meeting for Worship preceding our business meeting, the sound of snoring could be heard gradually increasing in volume. It was easy to identify the sleeping Friend, but not so easy to control one's expression as the snores reached a good bass note. No one knew quite what to do, as there were empty seats on either side of the tired one, and he was therefore out of reach of a friendly prod.

Suddenly the sleeper awoke, pulled a book out of his pocket, and informed us that he had been led to read that evening's texts from *Daily Light*. He obviously did not know he had been asleep, and he proceeded to read and expound upon—'Awake thou that sleepeth—It is high time to awake out of sleep'.

There is no doubt that that sermon will be remembered by those present long after many equally worthy ones are forgotten!'

Bees

In early days American farmers had much rough work to do and clothing was not easily obtained: so they were accustomed to wear leather breeches during the Winter. They were hung up in the attic during the warm summer months, to be ready for the autumn, when the frosts came. A revered Minister at Abington startled the meeting for worship one First-day by arising suddenly from the facing benches, proceeding with considerable speed down the aisle towards the door, and exclaiming, 'Friends, the Lord is in my heart, but the devil is in my breeches!'

A bee had crawled into his breeches in early autumn, and the warmth of his body had woken it when he donned his winter garments.

Slips of the Tongue

Considering that there is little speaking from notes in our Meetings for Worship, and that often those who take part acceptably are not practiced speakers in their other walks of life, it is remarkable how few slips of tongue occur, such as the dear Friend who prayed for people in every land and in the uninhabited parts of the earth!

Here is another example:

A speaker was telling the Meeting how in a time when he was ill and not able to work, he and his family had been saved by his cat bringing them rabbits. He concluded, 'And every day for forty days the cat brought that rabbit'.

Pot of Message

Edward Grubb told a story which lingered long in York Meeting of John Stephenson Rowntree's spoonerism, 'Jacob sold his birthright for a pot of message'. Feeling something wrong, he tried, 'message of', but finding that would not do, he altered it to 'That dish of animal food'.

Clothed

John Stephenson Rowntree was invited to preach in a Primitive Methodist Chapel; before he did so, the Minister prayed, 'O Lord, we thank thee that to-day the lecturer has come clothed and in his right mind!'

Caution

Caution and charity, even to the devil, were carried beyond ordinary limits by the Friend who spoke in Meeting of 'One who we are told was a liar from the beginning, and who, there is reason to fear, may not have been improved by age'.

Chaos

Eliza Kenworthy, who regularly spoke in York Meeting in the late 1920's on evangelical subjects, with a high tremulous voice, was known to that generation of scholars at Bootham and The Mount as 'Chaos'. This was because, on a well-remembered occasion, she had commenced with the quavering quotation, 'I am chaos, I am chaos.'

Not Heard

There was a period when some Quaker Ministers thought it impressive to stand in silence before beginning. An American visitor did this in a large Meeting, and a voice from a remote corner said, 'Our Friend is not heard'. To which the Minister replied, 'I h'aint said nothin' yet!'

Small Speaker

A Retreat patient listened to a visiting Friend of small stature, but of great fervour. When the visitor finished the patient rose, and said, 'Little pot, soon hot', and sat down.

Jump to It

When Mary Humphrey of Somerset was visiting Friends in the States, she was present as a Minister at a large Quarterly Meeting. Before she went in on Sunday morning, a local Friend drew her aside, and said, 'If thee has anything on thy mind to say, thee'll have to jump to it.' Needless to say, the vocal ministry did prove to be almost continuous.

Quaker Tramp

In the Yorkshire Dales, disownment for marrying out left closed Meeting Houses, but Quaker traditions. On a Quaker Tramp an old Yorkshire farmer, with Friend ancestry, was invited to a Meeting in the Old Meeting House. He replied, 'Why, mon, what's the good o' comin' to listen to fowks that 'as nowt to say?'

Hot Air

There was more than a ripple of laughter when the Clerk of the Churchtown Preparative Meeting, Dublin, was reading an expert's report on the condition of the Meeting House fabric and came to, 'There is hot air under the Ministers' Gallery'. Having worshipped in that helpful Meeting, I can vouch for the fact that this hot air had not caused any dry rot.

A Hen Enters

At a business meeting on a very hot afternoon, the door was left open. A hen walked in and proceeded steadily up the middle aisle towards the Clerk's desk. The Clerk asked, 'And what hast thou to lay before the meeting?'

Paul Not a Friend

Margaret Pike was expressing her high approval of women speaking in Meeting, and in public where it appeared desirable. Jonathan Pike remarked, 'Well, thee knows Paul was not of that opinion'. She replied with alacrity, 'But thee knows Paul was not a Friend!'

Embracing

When the Men's Meeting and the Women's Meeting met separately, the suggestion of joint meetings was being considered. One Quaker, supporting this, said, in all seriousness, that he was in favour of the Men Friends embracing the Women Friends.

Not Occurred to Him

A Committee was being appointed and a name was suggested by a Friend. A disapproving voice remarked, 'That is not a name which would have occurred to me'.

Those Who Speak Less Well

Roger Clark in his thanks to Birmingham Friends for their hospitality at the Birmingham Yearly Meeting, 1954, was at the top of his usual witty form. In one passage he said, 'I never know which to admire—

to envy—the most; the gifts—the skill—of those who speak well, and who delight us all; or the sheer courage of those who, shall I say, speak less well, but often at considerable length!'

Dan and Beersheba

Rufus Jones once lectured on his visit to the Holy Land in a small American township. Afterwards he was thanked by one of his audience who ended, 'Well folks, we've sure had a wonderful time. And to think until to-night I always thought that Dan & Beersheba were husband and wife, just like Sodom & Gomorrah!'

A Damaged Shoe

A young Friend, walking to a country Meeting in Dentdale one Sunday morning, knocked the cap of his shoe loose against the cobbles. They had four miles still to walk to the Meeting, and twenty miles in the afternoon to take in another Meeting.

His friend said, 'Why not go to a shoemaker?' The reply was that the only shoemaker was a Methodist local preacher, who would object to working on Sunday. However, the shoemaker was called upon and informed of the young Quaker's plight. A solemn pause ensued, then the local preacher, with a twinkle in his eye, said, 'If our Lord thought it right to help an ass get out of a hole on the Sabbath Day, I think I might mend thy shoe!'

Committees

Committees are most necessary, but can be rather futile.

Was it Rufus Jones who said, 'A Committee is a gathering of important people who singly can do nothing, but together can decide that nothing can be done.'

An even more scathing remark, by another Friend, was, 'The unwilling, chosen from the unfit, to do the unnecessary'.

The Friends in Council

Those who think of the days when men and women Friends wore Quaker dress as days of quiet seriousness for the Society should see if their Preparative Meeting Library contains, *The Friends in Council, a thin folio which can only be described as skittish.

It is about a Friends' First Day Schools' Conference in Darlington, which started '8th mo. 1st.', the year is not given but the Conference was held in 1874. The book ran into two editions.

The gathering was widely attended, for one picture is of three American Friends losing themselves in trying to find the Meeting House.

Yet another depicts the High Street, Darlington,

*See illustrations on pages 24, 74, 96, 110, taken from this folio and poem on page 128.

crowded with carts and hand-carts, bringing extra beds to Friends' House. Indeed Friends' hospitality was under such strain that the picture on page 74 shows what might have happened if more had sent in their names.

I also reproduce the Quaker coat of arms from the cover, as it is the only Friends' coat of arms I have ever seen.

Examples of the humour can be gathered from the following:—

8th mo., 3rd: Conference in the Meeting House: Subject 'Our Society On Its Last Legs'.

8th mo., 4th: Conference in the Meeting House: Subject 'How Long Will the Last Legs Last'.

Whilst the scale of the map of Darlington is somewhat cryptically stated to be—'One Friend's hat to a yard'.

CHAPTER IV

HISTORY: GRAVE AND GAY

When Was George Fox Born?

It is known that George Fox was born in July 1624 and that his birth was duly entered in the Parish Register at Fenny Drayton, but the exact day is not known. The reason for this is that about one hundred years after, the Sexton's wife was making jam. She could not find any paper for the tops of her jars and thought no-one would bother about entries of a century ago, so she tore out some of the older pages of the Parish Register. Thus, the exact date of George Fox's birth was lost in the process of jam making.

George Fox's Signature*

Examples of George Fox's full signature are rare. The one shown below is taken from an address to Charles II, preserved in a manuscript in London. George Fox's signings are almost always by initials, a sprawling 'g ff', or sometimes, even in print, merely 'G' or 'F.G.' This last has caused some confusion, but it is undoubtedly our George.

*Note how the double small 'f' signifies a capital 'F'.

Some Melancholy Thing

Pepys records in his Diary that 'Mr. William Penn, who is lately come over from Ireland, is a Quaker again, or some very melancholy thing!'

William Penn and Daylight Saving

William Penn set down rules for his family and household which show the modern Daylight Saving, without alteration of the clock:—

'That the family arise every morning from the first of the third month till the first of the fifth month about six in the morning, and from the first of the fifth month to the first of the ninth month about the fifth hour in the morning, and from the first of the ninth month to the first of the eleventh month about the sixth hour, and from the first of the eleventh month to the first of the third month about seven in the morning'.

We wonder how much latitude there was in that 'about'. Whether you got up at five or seven, breakfast was always at nine, and bed was always at ten.

Penn's Treaty With the Indians

Voltaire remarked of the Quaker Treaty with the Indians of Pennyslvania, that it was, 'the only Treaty that was ever concluded without an oath, and the only one that was never broken'.

It was doubtless owing to this success that President Grant, in 1869, seeking a solution of the troublesome Red Indian problem, turned over the administration of all the Indian tribes resident in Nebraska to the Society of Friends, and the Quakers took complete control for ten years.

The Way to Newgate

William Penn was often in prison for his faith. Once when he was again sentenced, the Captain of the Guard sent for soldiers to take him to prison. Said William Penn, 'Send for thy lacquey, I know the way to Newgate'.

Persecutions

It tells its own tale of Quaker persecutions to record simply that for many years the first three of the Yearly Meeting's queries were these:—

1. What present prisoners are there?
2. How many discharged since last year?
3. How many died prisoners?

And How Are They Attended?

In 1670 the first Meeting for 'Business' was held by Cork Quakers. It was held in the prison because most of the men Friends were there at the time.

Refusing the Oath

In 1661 a Proclamation was issued prohibiting meetings of Anabaptists, Quakers, and Fifth Monarchy Men, and commanding Justices to tender the Oath of Allegiance to persons brought before them for assembling at such meetings. As the Quakers would not take any oath, within a few weeks of the Proclamation 4,230 Quakers were sent to prison.

Not Marked

The most thrilling account in *Besse's Sufferings**
is of the man who was taken by the Press Gang on
Filey sands. At Portsmouth he and some others
attended a Quaker Meeting and became Quakers. They
had never heard of the peace testimony and, for a time,
the Captain found them the best fighting men he had
on board. Then it came to them that war and Quaker
principles were not in harmony, and they refused to
'haul the King's ropes'.

They were beaten, but such was their exaltation
that the Captain found no mark on them, so he
ordered the Quartermaster to be flogged for letting
them off so lightly.

Men's and Women's Sides

It is said that the reason for men and women sitting
on different sides of Meeting arose from the days of
persecution. The men sat on the door side, so that
they could walk out when soldiers arrived, leaving
the women to worship undisturbed.

'The Woodhouse'

That strange and bitter persecution of the Quakers
by the American Puritans was responsible for the

*Joseph Besse, schoolmaster, collected together and printed in
1753 in two thick folio volumes, details of the suffering of the
Quakers, in body, money or chattels. I can recommend them
to any Friend who is fortunate enough to find them amongst
old books in his Preparative Meeting Library.

building and voyage of 'The Woodhouse'. Because of the heavy fines on sea captains who took Quakers to America, no Friend could secure a passage. So George Fowler felt he must build a ship to take Quakers overseas. He built it, however, so small that neither captain or crew could be secured for the voyage. Nothing daunted, Fowler and eleven other Quakers, all without any experience of navigation, set sail for America. They escaped from storms, and even a fog saved them from capture by a warship. In about two months they arrived safely at their destination, although some were caught up in the persecution and ended their lives on the gallows.

The Quaker Envoy

The persecution of Friends in America was ended by Charles II sending a Quaker as his Envoy with orders that it should cease. Upon the Quaker coming covered before him, the Governor ordered his hat to be struck off. Then he had to restore the Quaker's hat, and remove his own, when he found he was standing before the King's Envoy.

Women Friends

How fearlessly the early Quaker women went about their Duty! Here is a record from Rebekah Butterfield's Diary which she began in 1671:

'Anne Gargill arrived in Lisbon from Plymouth in 1655, and went to the King's Palace. There she met an Irish Jesuit, and later others. She discoursed of religion freely, and even issued a paper against the

Popish religion, until she was finally summoned by 'The King's Chief General of his Land Forces and High Admiral at sea, and his Great Chamberlain and Keeper of the Privy Seal', and transported in the King's boat and the King's coach to the Palace of the Inquisition. For two hours twenty-five 'bishops', sitting about a table, examined her and heard her papers read, in which she declared against them and their idolatry, and called them Babylon and Anti-Christ! They tendered her a paper to sign to this effect, 'Not to come on Shoar again to that place, or to discourse with any of that Nation'. Yet upon her refusing to promise any such thing, she was returned to her ship with the same pomp, and without paying any of the expense.

My own comment is that this incident also shows the Inquisition in a very favourable light.

Relief

The earliest record* of Quaker Relief is a statement that Quakers in Dublin are said to have sent relief to the New England colonies in 1676 for those suffering from the wars with the Indians. It is, however, thought that 'Quakers in Dublin' is really a misrendering for 'Churches in Dublin'.

The earliest accepted record of Quaker Relief Work is the sending of food, and later money, from London to Philadelphia, for those suffering through the Revolutionary War.

*Diary of Increase by Mather, 1639-1723 (a puritan clergyman).

First Woman Preacher

In 1700, it was estimated that there were 9,500 Quakers in Jamaica. Elizabeth Hoolen who died there in 1671 had the distinction of being the first woman preacher in the Society of Friends.

Joseph Hewes

It is not correct to say that a Quaker was amongst those who signed the Declaration of American Independence. Joseph Hewes, whose signature is shown above, was a Quaker, but left the Society of Friends at the outbreak of the Revolution and so was not a Member of the Society at the time when he signed the Declaration.

Helping James II

Among the refugees helped by Friends was James II himself, who, when fleeing after the Battle of the Boyne, remembered a County Wexford Friend whom he had already met. The King sought help from this man, Francis Randall, who prevented his capture,

uncocked the pistols which the dejected monarch had
stuck loosely in his belt, gave him food, and sent his
son with fresh horses to guide James to the ship which
was waiting to carry him to France.

York Minster

It is said that an ancestor of the well-known Quaker
family of Fry offered Oliver Cromwell £400 to take
down York Minster. Fortunately the Lord Protector
wanted more!

A Schoolmaster Aspersed

Our Quaker schools and Friends in the teaching
profession may be interested in the following docu-
ment, showing how they were looked upon in 1679.
Certainly they could improve the spelling!

'Wee whose names are heerunto subscribed, being
Inhabitants of the Toune and parish of Whitby doe
humby certific that whereas we are informed, some
persons have cast an aspersion upon Mr. Christopher
Stephenson on whose behalf wee formerly Certified,
desireing that hee might have a license to teach
schoole in Whitby, that he is a noncormiss a consorter
with quakers and phanaticks, which was an obstruc-
tion to his proceedings in that good way of educating
children, which wee know to be false and a scandall
upon him, for that wee have seen him a constant
Church man both in Whitby and at Fylingdales ever
since his Coming to this parte of the countrie, and noe
consorter with phanaticks otherwise than all others
doe in ordinary Communicacion and to this we sett

our hands this 4 Aug. 1679.' (Then follow 28 signatures.)

Smoking Broadside

There is a broadside, undated, against the use of tobacco—whether ye worship in Smoke (tobacco), Dust (snuff) or in Pig-tail (chewing). The sheet is very practical. It disposes of the argument that smoking helps digestion thus: 'It is said that smoking and snuff relieve that uneasiness which arises from eating a too plentiful meal. A far more rational and effective remedy would be to eat less!'

Burning It Up Fast

Towards the close of the eighteenth century, American Friends seem to have been divided on the question of smoking. Two Ministers stole away after a Quarterly Meeting dinner at a Friend's house to enjoy their cigars on the back porch. Some Friends found them, and took them sharply to task. 'Yes, Friends', said John Hunt, 'It is a vile weed, and Samuel and I are burning it up as fast as we know how!'

Quakers in 'Punch'

On the verge of the outbreak of the Crimean War, Henry Pease and Joseph Sturge had a concern to visit the Czar, who received them well. The feeling in this country was against this visit, for Punch published a cartoon with a verse:

> Joseph Sturge
> Went to Urge
> Peace on the Emperor Nicholas,

Henry Pease
Crossed the seas
On the same errand ridiculous.

This is not the only Quaker cartoon in *Punch*, for John Bright was the subject of one or two, which included a picture showing John Bright, after having been appointed a Minister of the Crown, looking at himself in a long mirror, dressed in the court dress of his office, and wondering if he should wear it or his plain Quaker costume.

Parliament

Joseph Pease of Darlington was the first Quaker to enter Parliament. He was elected for South Durham in 1832 and caused the Clerks of the House some searching by claiming his Quaker right to affirm.

Archbishop of Canterbury

Robert Spence Watson was the power behind the throne in the Liberal Party in Gladstone's day. On the eve of Gladstone's final retirement from the office of Prime Minister, the two were considering the Honours List. When the work was completed, Gladstone said, 'As usual, Robert, your name is not down. You know, after your great services, you can have anything you want, anything!' Spence Watson replied, 'Well, there is one thing I would like'. Gladstone is said to have sat suddenly bolt upright, as he wondered what honour had at last attracted the sturdy Quaker, who up to then had always refused one. 'Yes, I would like to be Archbishop of

Canterbury'. Gladstone sat back with a snort, as he realized this was only a humorous way of refusing any honour.

Fighting

Joseph Brayshaw, when in prison as a Conscientious Objector, had a fellow prisoner who was in for assault on a policeman. 'Queer, ain't it', said the man, 'You're here for not fighting, and I'm here for fighting'!

Cautious Speech

President Hoover showed the cautious speech of his Quaker upbringing. A companion on a train journey remarked, 'Those sheep have been sheared.' To this, Hoover replied, 'Well on this side, certainly'.

Friends of the War

T. Edmund Harvey, whilst on relief work in France after the First World War, received two letters addressed as follows:

'Monsieur le Colonel Président de la Sociétè des Amis'.

'Sociétè des Amis de La Guerre'.

Let the Devil Roar

Mark Guy Pearse, a famous Wesleyan Minister, once said of the late nineteenth century Quakers, 'They sat quiet in their Meeting Houses, and let the devil roar outside'.

Druids

Heard in an air-raid shelter: 'They're Quakers, you know, descended from the Druids'.

Quaker Stamps

Professor Maurice A. Mook, in an article in *The Friends Journal*, drew attention to the Quaker stamps which have been issued, and, although they are mostly American Stamps and not British, Friends this side of the Atlantic may be interested in his list.

The first to be issued by the U.S.A. depicted William Penn. Then followed one of Susan B. Anthony the Women's Suffrage leader, whose later portrait appeared years after on a 50 cent stamp. The poet Whittier was included in an American poets series, and Lucretia Moll appeared drawn with Quaker cap with two non-Friends, recording 100 years of women's progress. The Quaker cap also appears in a German stamp of Elizabeth Fry. The Japanese Quaker states-man, Dr. P. My Nibola, is shown on a Japanese stamp. Then there is a Norwegian stamp which pictures the sloop Restoration and Cleng Pearson who led a party of Quakers from Norway to seek religious freedom in the U.S.A. This ship is also shown in a two cent American stamp.

There are some stamps of born Friends who in later life left the Society. Nathaniel Greene, who resigned so that he could fight with Washington; J. Fenimore Cooper, whose exciting boys' tales I read when I was young; Edward A. Macdowell, the composer; and David Boone, who did so much to open up the West. Nor should one forget Betsy Ross, who is depicted showing her flag to Washington. She had an unusual experience: she was disowned for marrying Ross, who was not a Quaker, but for her third husband she married a Quaker and was readmitted. For 72 years she was a Quaker and for 20 years she was not.

Any Friend who is a stamp collector (plain speech for a philatelist) may like the Stanley Gibbons numbers; they are in the order given above:

U.S.A., 898: 929: 1199: 1000: & 1106. GERMANY, 1082. JAPAN, C.203. NORWAY, 388. U.S.A., 840: 930: 995: 1017: 1046: 1157: 1002 & 1013. TURKEY, 1179. U.S.A. 853 1244: 847: 1285: & 1285a.

SLEEPING ACCOMMODATION

ILLUSTRATION FROM 'THE FRIENDS IN COUNCIL'

CHAPTER V

ODDITIES

Sleeping Accommodation

The wording under the picture in the Darlington Book* is as follows:

'Although all doors were open to receive Friends in Darlington, it was not found quite so easy to supply every individual with a bed. Thence the peculiar position taken by Friends in our sketch; one dear young Friend with a horror of rats, sweetly slumbered on three towel horses and suffered much from nightmares; another Friend reposed on a wash stand and dream't he was a piece of soap; a third Friend slept with his head on Besse's *Sufferings†* and *Youthful Pilgrims,* which caused him to dream that he was gathered young and was reading his own obituary notice in the *Annual Monitor* commencing in the usual way, 'This dear young Friend from early youth evinced': two enterprising Friends got into a large carpet bag and then hung themselves on a peg in the wall.'

The Horse Was Going to Meeting

John Wilhelm Rowntree, when on a visit to America, was being driven the six miles or so to Meeting one Sunday in a one-horse buggy. Part way there the horse balked. John Wilhelm Rowntree's host gave him the reins, got down, and went to the animal's head. He took the bridle in both hands, lifted the horse's head and addressed it—'Waal

The Friends in Council.   †See footnote page 64.

Thomas! thee thinks thee's not going to Meeting—
I think thee *is* going—I know thee, and thee knows me.
I ain't going to thrash thee, and I'ain't going to cuss
thee, and I'll give thee just two minutes, and if thee
doesn't move on then, I WILL TWIST THY
DARNED TAIL'. He remounted the buggy, and
after two minutes began the operation—and the
horse moved on.

The Quaker's Cow

The Quaker's cow had kicked over the milk
bucket, and then, when the farmer had partly filled
it again, it was kicked over once more. The Friend
rose from his milking stool, took the cow by the
horns, and thus addressed it: 'Thee knows I am a
Quaker and can'st not swear at thee; thee knows as a
Quaker I can'st not beat thee; but what thee dost not
know is that I am selling thee to a Baptist to-morrow,
and then thee will have to look out for thyself!'

The next series illustrates that words sometimes
can be taken to mean something other than their
writers intended.

An Agony Column

Kenneth Brown, in a letter to *The Friend*, suggested
that the paper might have an Agony Column, because
he wondered if advertisers always secured what they
wanted.

He instanced the request for 'an abstainer (part-
time)', wondered if that for a 'resilient female' got
more than he bargained for, and thought the poor

caravan which was 'entirely alone' sounded pathetic. He added that an advertisement of his own for a cottage to let, 'Bath 8 miles' was true, whichever way one took it.

A Black Eye

A Friend was making a dress, and ran short of one small item, so she went to a neighbour and asked, 'Wilt thou be so kind as to give me a black eye?' Neighbour, 'Well! I am surprised! I should be sorry to believe myself capable of doing any such thing!' Explanations followed, the request was granted, and the dress completed.

Christians Next Door

The Society of Friends' building was next to that of the Society of Jews and Christians. There was some confusion between the two, so outside the Quaker Dining Room a notice was put up, 'Jews and Christians feed next door'.

Friends' Casino

Two foreign visitors enquired for 'The Friends House Casino'. It transpired that they really wanted 'The Friends House Canteen'.

Illness

A Meeting House Yard Notice read: 'Overseers would be glad to hear of cases of illness'.

Mass Delivery

Statement in a Yearly Meeting, 'We went round delivering 25,000 leaflets to every house'.

New Patient

When Robert O. Mennell came the evening before his first Committee, he thought he would like to see how new patients were received at The Retreat. He therefore asked the Medical Superintendent to admit him as a patient, and not to say anything to those who would take charge of him. Robert Mennell was therefore admitted.

Robert afterwards praised the kindly and efficient way he was received, and all went well until he wanted to get up to attend Committee. The difficulty Robert had had to persuade the Doctor to admit him was as nothing to the difficulty he had to persuade the Nurse that he was a member of Committee. It was a new one to the Nurse; he had heard of a patient who thought he was Lord Nelson, and on the first morning had demanded his full-dress uniform for an official call on the Lord Mayor. The nurse used all his skilled training to take the mind of the 'patient' from his 'delusion', but this 'patient' was unusually persistent. Fortunately the Doctor remembered his 'patient' and to the great relief of both 'patient' and nurse, Robert attended his Committee.

The Male Nurse

A somewhat dangerous Retreat patient escaped, and some male nurses were sent to find him. In the course of their search they naturally told the neighbouring farmers for whom they were looking. One male nurse had long hair, and the day being windy, he looked rather wild. Some farmers captured him.

He told them who he was, but they only soothed him by saying the doctor would settle that. Thus in the tight grip of two burly farmers he was brought before the Medical Superintendent! He was advised to cut his hair.

Record Floods

William H. Sessions, after being seventeen years Honorary Treasurer of The Retreat, had to ring up to ask the way there. This sounds like inattention to duty for seventeen years, but was not. Record floods had almost cut York in two. The Treasurer knew the dry way from his house into the City, but not that out of the City to The Retreat.

Fairly Soon

The Yorkshireman loves understatement; nothing is ever 'good', it is only 'fairly good'. At a York Schools' Committee there had been recorded in our Yorkshire fashion that something be done 'fairly soon'. A Friend, not of Yorkshire, queried this, and said he was sure the Committee had decided it to be done 'soon', and asked, 'am I being finickity?'. Said the Yorkshire Chairman, John Harvey, 'fairly finickity'!

Alarming Telegram

During one of Bevan Braithwaite's continental travels about 1872, he was taken very ill in Athens. His family at home received an alarming telegram from his daughter, 'Father strangled, mother executed': on further enquiry they found the telegram ought to have read, 'Father stronger, mother expected.'

Penn's City

I wonder if the early Quaker settlers and their relatives at home found difficulty in spelling the name of Philadelphia? I came across a Family Bible in which a good old yeoman Yorkshire farmer, of uncertain schooling, had been faced with the task of recording that his brother had died in this City. He spelt it 'Phillidelfiah'. The spelling is quaint, but the sound is as near to correctness as that of the school boy who spelt 'Eau de Cologne'—'Oh Dick alone'.

Swarthmore College

Swarthmore College in America secured a gift of $100,000 and the new president, Frank Aydelotte, expected the news to be received with immediate enthusiasm. He reckoned without Quaker reticence, for the news was received in silence, until broken by a Friend who quietly remarked, 'I see no reason why we should not accept the gift'.

A Cooling of Temper

John William Hall of Thirsk once had an apprentice who was a nice young fellow, except for his temper. Once J.W.H. came into his shop to find a row going on between his son and the apprentice, whose fiery temper was at its height. J.W.H. quietly said, 'Alfred, follow me!' He was led to a lavatory and told to take off his coat, whilst J. W. Hall filled the basin from the cold tap. Then, with a quiet—'Bend down', Alfred's head was firmly pressed into the bowl. 'There'—said J.W.H., 'dry thyself, put on thy coat, and go back into the shop. Thou wilt find thou art cooler now.' Alfred's temper sometimes came on top after this, but it only needed John William Hall to appear for it to quieten down.

Quaker Caution

One Quaker said to another, 'Was not Thomas thy Grandfather?' He replied, 'I am told so'.

An Edward Grubb Story

A letter from Edward Grubb to a niece reads, 'I hope you will manage your house cleaning without getting knocked up, and that the sweep will prove amenable. Did you hear of the swearing sweep, who was converted by the Salvation Army, and was holding forth at a meeting about how he had been notably changed. 'I was sweeping a chimney the other day, and the brush stuck, it wouldn't go up, and it wouldn't go down. Did I swear? No, my friends, I shouted, "Praise the Lord", and the bloody brush went up like smoke!'

A Lovely Complexion

From *Saintly Lives* comes a charming story:—

A dear old Quakeress, who was asked what gave her such a lovely complexion and what cosmetics she used, replied sweetly, 'I use for the lips truth, for the voice prayer, for the eyes pity, for the hands charity, for the figure uprightness, and for the heart love!'

The Mayflower

A Friend's new daily help said, 'You, a Quaker! I thought the Quakers went to America in the *Mayflower*, and are all dead now!'

Quaker Ages

A Dalesman going round an old Quaker graveyard, remarked on the great age of the early Friends buried there, 87, 85, 83, 77 and so on. Then he came to a stone which gave the age 45, whereupon he remarked, 'He wad likely not be born and bred a Quaker. He'd be a convert!'

Birthdays

At a Guest House the general conversation turned on birthdays. A Friend was asked when her's was, but she shook her head. Later she quietly remarked to her nearest neighbour, 'On the eighteenth day of eight month, in the year eighteen eighty eight, I was eighteen!'

Our Peace Testimony

The Times published an amusing Quaker story.

The Captain of the trawler was listening on the wireless to some selections from the comic opera, 'The Quaker Girl', and he said, 'Blood-thirsty people those Quakers, they steal up to you in the dark, and kill you with their knives!'

Said the wireless operator, 'You mean Gurkas, not Quakers'. The Captain of the trawler, not liking to be corrected by the young wireless operator—'Oh! well, they are both as bad as one another!'

Dost Thou?

Herman Melville tells us in *Moby Dick*—

'He says he's our man, Bildad', said Peleg, 'He wants to ship'. 'Dost thee?' said Bildad, in a hollow voice, and turning round to me. 'I dost', said I unconsciously, he was so intense a Quaker.

I'll Get Him

A Friend wanting a dog was recommended to a dealer, whose reputation was not so good as his knowledge of the points of a dog. Stating in full detail the exact kind of dog he wanted, the Quaker was interrupted by the dealer saying, 'Look 'ere, Mister, tell me whose dog it is you want, and I'll get 'im for you'.

Quaker Cheque

In the days of plain speech, a man forged a Quaker's cheque. This was so skilfully done that the cashier was about to pay, when he noticed that in the date was the name of the month, whereas the Quaker always put its number, and so the forger was trapped.

Watch and Pray

After thieves had ransacked the cloakrooms of Devonshire House, Friends found written up outside the Old Meeting House, 'Friends should watch as well as pray!'

A Wrong Impression of Us!

How some others see us is illustrated by the following: When a Quaker child is born, the father or some near relative takes it in his arms, and exclaims, 'Welcome to this vale of misery!'

Feeble Frames

Arnold S. Rowntree was a big man in both senses of the word, his nick-name amongst the children at the York Friends Schools being 'Chocolate Jumbo'. He once caused some amusement at a Peace Meeting in Manchester by speaking about 'our feeble frames' while leaning with his full weight on the Elders' gallery partition, until its creaking could be heard in protest.

Where Thee Standeth

A gentle Quaker, hearing a strange noise in his house, got up and discovered a burglar busily at work. So he went quietly and got his gun, then came back and stood in the doorway. 'Friend', he said, 'I would do thee no harm for the world, but thee standeth where I am about to shoot'.

The Cost of Transportation

An ancestor of mine was so sturdy a Quaker resister that he was finally sentenced to be transported. It has always struck me that it was rather mean of the Judge to fine him also £30, 'To cover the cost of the transportation.' He died in York Castle before the sentence could be carried out. There is, however, no record

in the family of the £30 fine being refunded, despite
its specific object.

Quaker Oats

In a campaign in the First World War an order was
given that the religion should be put on the Identity
Discs. It was a kindly thought, so that wounded men
could be visited by padres of their own faith.

A member of the F.A.U. came up to give his
particulars, and said his religion was Quaker. Said
the sergeant in charge, 'That's not a religion, it's a
trade mark'.

The Backhouses of Darlington

At a Darlington Exhibition there was a bronze
statue of the Greek God Bacchus in the entrance hall.
It was a beautiful work of art, and a sculptor was most
intrigued in seeing the keen interest in which two
men, evidently tough miners, were examining the
statue. He strolled up to them and asked if they
were interested in sculpture or art. One of them
replied, 'Nay! We know nowt about them; we was
capped (puzzled) to know which Backus (the local
pronunciation of Backhouse) this were. E's like
none of them we ken, an' my mate were just saying
" 'e 'asn't right kind of Backus jib (face)" '.

J.T.Wilson. 1860.

At Hill's the Confectioners—A Snack during Yearly Meeting, 1860.

CHAPTER VI

CHILDREN

A Dog Holds a Meeting

L. Violet Holdsworth told a delightful children's dog story in *The Friends Quarterly Examiner* of January 1936. I can give only the bare details here.

'The Collie of Hoonaze Ware' seems to be a Quaker story which has been handed down in the Society. Is it true? Violet Holdsworth says she believes it is a true story because it was told her by a very truth-telling Friend, who remembered hearing it when she was a little girl from her mother, who always told true narratives to her children.

The story is of a Meeting in a large village; all the worshippers were old, because the younger Friends had settled in the towns. One by one the old people died, until the only ones to come to Meeting were a farmer and his dog, who lay during the meeting at the feet of his master. Then the old farmer died. The next Sunday the collie was seen coming to Meeting as usual. When he found the door locked, he howled and howled, so the neighbours took the key off the nail to let him in. True to his sheep dog instinct, he ushered them into seats, then lay down in his usual place. When the neighbours rose to go out, the dog growled so much that they sat down again quietly, until the church clock chimed the usual time for meeting to end, when the dog rose and the strange meeting was over. The next Sunday more people were there, curious to see 'the farmer's dog hold a Meeting'. The third Sunday there were still more, and a visiting Friend, doubting if there was a Meeting at all, looked in and found more people there than he had ever known before. He preached to them of the Quaker faith, and the living silence of a Friends' Meeting. Some of those who had come from curiosity found the silence restful to their hearts, and to others the preacher's words came home, so these came Sunday after Sunday. Thus the farmer's collie did more than hold a Meeting, he restarted it.

The Fatted Calf

I love the kindliness of the little girl's answer to the question, 'Who was sorry when the Prodigal son returned!' She said, 'The fatted calf!'

Dear Friend

As a small boy I liked going to Harrogate Monthly Meeting with my mother, for Jane Pickard would take me home after morning Meeting for Worship, and devote herself to my enjoyment. So pleased was I at her kindness that I begged to write her a letter of thanks, all on my own. I took the letter, in its childish writing and sketchy spelling, to my father to be addressed and stamped. He chuckled as he read it, took up his pen to make an alteration, but put it down, saying, 'No! it will give more enjoyment as it is'. The letter started, 'Dear Fiend!'

Nursery Rhymes

It is well known that early Friends altered Latin grammars to avoid pagan examples, but V. Sackville-

West, in her delightful book on *Nursery Rhymes*, states that the Quakers altered these too. She has kindly allowed me to reproduce the extract, but wrote that although she carefully put down in her notes for her book the references, there is no reference down about this Quaker one. Here is V. Sackville-West on 'The Cat and the Fiddle'.

'A very peculiar jingle, very peculiar indeed, in fact nonsensical; and so the Quakers thought, for they tried to amend it. They tried to turn it into reasonable sense, which is the last thing any child desires. Re-arranged by the Quakers this is how the old rhyme came out.

'Hey diddle diddle, The cat and the fiddle'

(Yes, thee may say that, for that is nonsense)

'The cow jumped over the moon'

(Oh no, Mary, thee mustn't say that, for it is falsehood, thee knows a cow could never jump over the moon; but a cow may jump under it; so thee ought to say,

The cow jumped *under* the moon)

'The little dog laughed. . . .'

(Oh, Mary, stop! How can a little dog laugh? Thee knows a little dog can't laugh. Thee ought to say, The little dog barked. . . .)

'And the dish ran after the spoon. . . .'

(Stop, Mary, stop! A dish can never run after a spoon. Thee had better say. . . .)

I have asked a number of Friends with long Quaker traditions in their families, but have not heard of any editing of Nursery Rhymes. I also asked Professor Mook, who has done a great deal of research in American Friends' folklore, but he had not heard of any. We both put letters in our respective country's Friends' Journals on the subject, but received only negative replies.

It is evident that V. Sackville-West has come across at least one strict Quaker family who altered Nursery Rhymes, but this cannot have been at all general.

There must have been some selection; there was plenty of scope for it, as the Opies* in their book of Nursery Rhymes give 550 different ones. It is impossible to consider a mother, coming from a Women's Meeting which had condemned following vain fashions and allowing curls to escape from under Quaker caps, then teaching her child—

> There was a girl in our town,
> Silk an' satin was her gown
> Silk an' satin, gold an' velvet,
> Guess her name, three times I've telled it.
>
> or
>
> There was a little girl, and she had a little curl,
> Right in the middle of her forehead;
> When she was good, she was very, very good,
> But when she was bad, she was horrid.

'Larned' to Sit Still

How would modern children like to go to Sunday School from 9.15 to 10.15 and then, after a quarter of

*See also page 124.

an hour's break, sit in Meeting from 10.30 to 12.0 o'clock.

I went through this, but was so restless in Meeting that I was put back for six months before being tried again.

Indeed I was put back four times, so it took me two years to qualify, being a lively youngster. (My father is said to have told my mother:—'Mary, it will take our united endeavour to bring up this boy!')

In Praise of Christian Parents

Kathleen Carrick Smith, writing under the above title in *The Friend* has some good children's stories.

A little boy's prayer: 'Thank you for abling me to slide down the clothes-post!'

Another, 'I want to thank God for Daddy, because he's always ordinary!'

Little girl playing in the garden said to an intrusive and persistent puppy—'O, go away! What with you and God following me about, I can't do a thing!'

Swearing

A Bishop was examining a class in the religious views of different sects, but no one could tell him about the Quakers. He said, 'Surely boys you know the difference between a Quaker and myself?' One boy then replied, 'Please, my Lord, a Quaker doesn't swear!'

Holy Bible

Ellen C. Waller was checking up the children's Bibles, to see that they all had the Revised Version, from which she was working. One child said, 'I'm afraid my Bible is wrong, it's not 'Revised', its 'Holy!'

God is a Spirit

The Friends' Temperance Union Secretary started an address at Ayton School by asking the juniors if any of them could quote a text from the Bible about strong drink. There was silence, then a small boy put up a quivering hand, and said, 'God is a Spirit'.

Quaker Howler

Four crockets make one Quaker.

A Two-Way Prayer

A little Quaker child was heard to pray, 'Please God help us to be good to-morrow; and if we're not, help Mummy not to be so cross with us'.

God's Name

A wee lassie said at a Friends' Mission, 'I know God's name, it is our Father Wishart, Harold be thy name.'

Minuet

A neat Friend howler is: 'In Quaker business meetings the Clerk often writes a minuet, to help to keep Friends in step.' Frankly I suspect the last seven words to be an addition!

Lamb or Mutton

Stephen Grellet, the French Quaker, was addressing the girls at Mountmellick. He intended to refer to them as 'little lambs', but missed his translation, and called them 'little muttons'.

Surprise for the Footman

Arnold S. Rowntree, as a curly-headed little boy, was taken to a party at a stately home. He swarmed up the liveried form of a footman, declaring—'Me does love oo!'

Anything to Say

A boy of six was taken to Meeting for the first time. His Mother had been careful to explain to him that the Meeting would be held largely in silence, though anyone present who felt called to speak would do so. The Meeting began with a long period of quiet. Eventually the boy whispered, 'Mother, have you anything to say to the Meeting?' Mother said softly, 'I don't think I have'. 'I don't think I have either,' said the boy, 'Let's get up and go'.

Unwanted Baby

An English Friend was travelling in Ireland on his own. There was a woman with a baby and a number of parcels in the compartment. She suddenly found the train was stopping at a junction where she ought to change. She gave the baby to the Friend to hold, and although the train had begun to move, a porter got the woman and her parcels out, and shut the door. In this way the Friend was left with a baby in arms. However, at the next station he persuaded the caretaker of the Ladies Cloak-room to take the baby, and wired to the junction to say what he had done.

A Run-Away Ring

Elizabeth Gurney Dimsdale, in long silk dress and Quaker bonnet, saw some urchins trying to ring a house bell, so she kindly rang it for them. They immediately ran away! After a moment's hesitation, she too ran away.

Quack, Quack

A solicitor in York, who started life as a poor boy, was told that if he followed the boys of the Quaker school on the way from the Meeting House, shouting 'Quack! Quack!', they would give him a new suit of clothes. So the ragged urchin went after the Bootham boys, shouting 'Quack! Quack! Quack!' at the top of his voice, until he could shout no longer. Alas! no suit of clothes appeared. I remember in my younger days the old solicitor was one of the neatest dressed men in York. He used to tell this tale, and with sly humour declare that the Quakers still owed him a suit of clothes.

Hair Cut

Child, 'Do Quakers never take off their hats to anyone?' Mother, 'I believe not, dear'. Child, 'Then how do they get their hair cut?'

Kindly Aunt

A kindly Aunt wrote inviting one of her four school-boy nephews to stay with her. On his arrival she asked, 'And how did thee decide who was to come?' 'We tossed for it, Aunt'. 'And you won?' 'No, Aunt, I lost!'

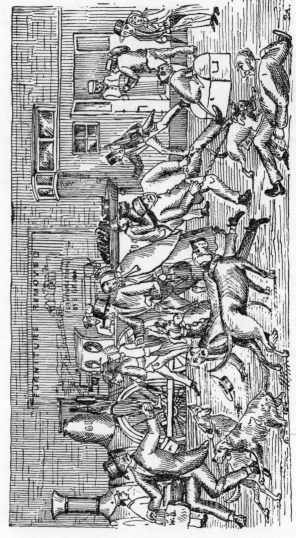

Arrival of Friends at Darlington and Simultaneous Departure of Dog Show.

CHAPTER VII

QUAKER SCHOOLS

The Friends First Day School Conference at Darlington in 1874 had a most inauspicious beginning. It is related under the picture opposite.

Now it came to pass that as Conference Friends poured out of the train at Darlington, a large party of eminent Dogs, returning home from the show, were waiting to pour into it. The Confusion that ensued was terrible, one dear young Friend was eaten up alive and nothing left but his collar carefully marked; the Box of George and Elizabeth Bottomlea was invaded by a ferocious little animal of most forbidding aspect, who settled permanently on the lid, using language of the most stalwart description, whilst they gazed in Horror from afar off.

Dante and George Fox

Bootham School had busts of Dante and George Fox. These formed an irresistible attraction for the boys. School caps were put on them at rakish angles, moustaches were drawn on, varying from that of a cavalry officer to a drooping walrus one. They appeared with cigarettes in their mouths. One ingenious boy fitted up Dante with a dummy cigarette which glowed at the end by means of a battery. The busts were therefore put on high, but it became a recognised 'mountain climb' to decorate the busts.

One day, George Fox was seen with a black eye, and admirers of this new decoration were told it was the result of George having a fight with Dante. After that the busts were withdrawn, and George Fox and Dante presumably now live in peace and darkness.

A. Neave Brayshaw

On one of his famous archaeological excursions, A. Neave Brayshaw (always known by his nickname of 'Puddles') cheered his sea-sick Bootham boys, anding at St. Malo with 'Laddies, remember Romeo & Juliet. "The stories of our woes shall furnish sweet discourse for time to come"!'

Puddles in Goal

It may surprise even some Bootham Old Scholars to know that Neave Brayshaw once played in goal. The Old Scholars had turned up two short, and so two masters offered to make up the team. Puddles let six goals through, a fact which, I am sure everyone will agree, showed very poor cover by the backs, and too forward play by the centre-half!

He Came Third

Neave Brayshaw had a very distinctive speech, and once at a re-union there was a competition behind a screen of the best imitators. Neave was persuaded to compete, but only came third!

Onion Washing

Don Thorp was maintenance officer at Bootham School, York for many years, and related the following:

'I have been asked to do some queer things in my time at Bootham. I think the queerest of all was when I was a youth and the late Mrs. Arthur Rowntree asked me if I would wash the paint work in the drawing room of 49, while they were away. She insisted on it being washed with onion water. One bucket of that was enough for me! I washed the rest with soap and water, and the day she was due back I boiled some onions in the room. She was delighted when she saw and smelt it!'

Parents and Teachers

Comment of a master on a school boy, 'Dull, but steady; would make a good parent!'

Here by contrast is a story my daughter Anne tells of her teaching days. A mistress bounced into the Common Room, after a hectic interview with a mother, exclaiming, 'The only people who ought not to have children are parents!'

The same problem was expressed by a former Head of Bootham, in a different way, 'There are moments when I feel that in the next world I would like to be Head Master of an Orphanage'.

Askham Bog

The natural history boys of Bootham School have always been interested in Askham Bog. One day in the village, on the way to the Bog, a man in a gig asked some of the boys the name of the place. They said, 'Askham'. The man thundered, 'Ask who, you fools?' and drove on.

The Pellet of Soap

One night at Bootham the boys of a bedroom were trying to drop pellets of soap on the passers by. One pellet hit with a ping the top of a bowler hat. The man looked up, saw the boys looking out of the window, shook his fist at them, and, with apparent anger, rang the front door bell loudly. All the next day the boys expected to have to appear before authority because of the incident, but nothing happened. They therefore asked the maid, who attended to the front door, if a caller had come about the time of their pellet throwing. 'Oh, yes' said the maid, 'a gentleman called and asked if Mr. Jeremy Jones lived here? I told him, he did not. I think he was having me on, because he was laughing to himself as he turned away'.

Truly Irish

Hubert Lidbetter, born in Dublin, was relating an incident at Bootham School and concluded, 'It happened while I was there, but I wasn't there when it happened!'

Charades

At a time when the older and stricter Friends disapproved of acting, the Bootham end of term entertainments were termed 'charades'. They were surely very ambitious charades, for they included some of Shakespeare's plays.

In one charade a Macbeth witch fell off the platform and was caught and replaced by Donald Gray, and had immediately to answer the question, 'Where hast thou been, sister?'

John A. Kay adds, 'since when Bootham has never taken Macbeth quite seriously'.

Cork and Water

Elizabeth Woodhead, called by the boys, 'Betty Lumber', 'Timber Toes', and 'Cork and Water' was housekeeper at Bootham School some seventy or eighty years ago. She dosed the boys for minor ailments and had one sovereign remedy for everything, according to the boys, 'from a broken leg to a common cold'. It was a colourless liquid and was known as 'cork and water', and I believe was still used for years after Elizabeth Woodhead left.

Sardines and Condensed Milk

Brian Sparkes related the story of his going into the box room at Bootham, and seeing a pallid young boy, about whose health the staff were worried, sitting on his tuck-box with an open tin of sardines and an open tin of condensed milk. This weakly schoolboy was to be seen picking up a sardine by the tail, dipping it into the condensed milk, and transferring the whole sardine, thus garnished, to his mouth!

Joining the Navy

Commander Gurney Braithwaite, in a humorous speech at a Bootham Old Scholars gathering, declared it was Arthur Rowntree's scripture lessons which made him join the Navy. Arthur Rowntree looked up in surprise. Gurney Braithwaite was by no means abashed, and said it was a vivid account of 'the Widow's cruise'!

Interrelated

The ban on 'marrying out' led to Quakers being rather interrelated, so that when a Bootham boy received an invitation to tea with his cousin, who had just left The Mount, permission was refused, but when they remembered they were also aunt and nephew, no-one demurred and the outing took place.

The Mount School and Burglars

The first burglary was in 1850 when a burglar entered the premises and carried off the plate basket, containing a large number of spoons, 'chiefly of German silver, but some of real silver'.

The second burglary was in 1862. A policeman saw two men crossing the field by the house and pursued them; they dropped a bag containing the silver they were carrying. He picked it up, then returned and roused the household by loudly ringing the front door bell. This was answered by two men issuing from the house, who had a scuffle with him on the door step, and then made their escape.

The third burglary was in 1957, when a girl noticed a shadowy form and tackled the burglar. As he was in his stocking feet he slipped on the polished floor and tumbled down. Before he could get up, the door was blocked with girls, so he quickly surrendered and the police were brought.

The accuracy of Head Mistresses does cramp the style of the collector of stories! The newspapers are much more picturesque. The description of the 1862 burglary was that, 'some forty of the young ladies, on the first alarm, rushed into the kitchen, and strangled two of the robbers!' The 1957 newspaper report was milder, but it said, 'eight of the girls tackled the burglar, got him down, and sat on him until the police arrived!'

Faithful in Little

The Mount School motto is, 'Fidelis in Parvo'.

One junior girl translated it, 'Faithful little things'.

The Daily Text

At The Mount School, York, a short passage, chosen by the Head, was until recent times learned and recited aloud by a girl each day at breakfast.

Last century, the morning text was always biblical, and was chosen by the girl who had to repeat it.

One day a girl chose a verse from the Psalms, 'I have more understanding than all my teachers'. After that the passage was selected by the Head Mistress!

Duchesses

Dr. Kitching, then head of The Retreat, had invited some Mount School girls to tea. They were out on the lawn in front of the house, when a military-looking patient approached, and bowing to each with courtly grace, addressed them each in turn, separately, as duchesses of counties of England. There was a Duchess of York, of Derby, etc., and then turning to the smallest—'And you, Madam, are the Duchess of Rutland'!

Infective Yawns

Pictures of Mount School girls of old make them look very demure and proper to present-day eyes. Were they? One incident related in *The Mount School History* seems to suggest not. The incident is related thus: 'Then there was that conspiracy of the youngest girls on the front forms; a conspiracy openly repressed by the senior girls, but covertly enjoyed, as they watched from their back rows a contagion of yawning pass along the ministerial benches, attacking one revered Friend after another, Minister, Elder, Overseer. They knew the front-bench rascals were at their game of ostentatious, albeit apparently smothered yawns whenever a glance from the heads of Meeting strayed in their direction. This usage was defended by the young ones on the ground of fair play, being practised only when Meeting time was legitimately up.

Hoshangabad

A collecting box for the Indian orphan, for whose upkeep The Mount School subscribed, was in the staff room. An unwilling member of the staff covered the box with a duster. Five minutes later, H. Winifred Sturge put up the following verse she had written:

'There was a school marm in a fluster,
Who covered a box with a duster.
No pence to be had for Hoshangabad,
Nor sixpence for orphans who trust her!'

Gas Brackets

At Ackworth we discovered that the gas brackets had a little 'play' and by moving them up and down long enough the other lights, even on the girls' side, flickered. It was good fun whilst it lasted, although it caused a great deal of trouble to the man in charge of the school gas works, in unsuccessfully trying to trace the cause. It was traced, however, by a master who caught us in the act, and we, and not the gas, were suitably treated!

April Fool

A new Master came in the middle of the first half (terms had not come in then), and naturally the boys tested him out. One boy shouted out, 'Ball up, Sir'. As it was the first of April there was no ball to be seen. The boy was called up, lectured for trying to make a fool of the master, and told to write out the Sixth Latin Declension ten times. The new master's stock fell badly in the five minutes the boys were assembling for the next class. All sorts of things were said about a master who couldn't take a joke on the first of April. Then one boy, who knew a little more Latin than the rest, said, 'I don't believe there is a Sixth Declension'. There was a rush for Latin grammars. When the boys found the April Fool joke was on them, the stock of the new master rose rapidly.

Boxed on the Ear

Frederick Andrews used to relate that when head boy of the school at fourteen years of age, he was asked to take the place of the youngest teacher apprentice, who had left suddenly. He said, 'I picked a quarrel with the biggest of my form of small boys, and boxed his ears—the prerogative, as it seemed to me, of full authority as a teacher. The boy was a wag, and dropped to the ground, seemingly senseless as a stone. Oh, the agony of that moment! Eugene Aram's fiat flashed into my mind—a coroner's inquest at the outset of my teaching career! How tenderly I raised that boy! How I hugged him for 'having me on'. It was a lesson, for in my subsequent half-century of teaching, I never transgressed so again.'

Gesture in Speech

F.A. was a fine speaker, and I still well remember a lecture on speaking which he gave to the Literature Class. He was illustrating gesture, and said, 'Beware of the open hand, lest you do this to your audience.' We just gasped when we saw the Head—*the Head!* making for a moment 'a nose' at us. The rest of the school found it hard to believe our story when we came out of the Literature Class.

Noses

When my children were at The Mount Junior School, they came home with a skit on one of their teachers, which, though not admitted to them, I thought was very neatly put for the scholars of a junior school. I found out, however, it was not original, but a parody of something much older, for E. H. Bennis gives the same jingle with a different name. I had better give the Bennis version!

'Bassett's nose is long.
Bassett's nose is strong,
'Twere no disgrace to Bassett's face
If Bassett's nose was gone.'

The little imps of The Mount Junior School scored, however, in the last line, for their version was neater. It ran:

'If half her nose was gone.'

Liver

A rough maid was setting dishes of liver at each end of the long tables at Penketh School. There came a crash, and the maid rushed out of the dining room crying, 'The boys' livers are on the floor!'

Lost Purse

The parents of a new boy at Sidcot School complained to the Head that when their son had lost his purse, the class master had not helped him, indeed he had sworn at him. Strict investigation followed, and it was found that Helen Hunt was the teacher to whom the finder of any lost property gave it.

All the Master had said to the boy about his lost purse was, 'Go to Helen Hunt for it!'

Usage

Robert Martin Lidbetter, in his school in Dublin, had a boy who spelt 'usage' phonetically correctly, but without a single correct letter in it, as follows: YOOZITCH.

Prayer

A boy at Leighton Park School let his handkerchief fall; in trying to recover it he fell on his knees, and the meeting rose. Sizing up the awkward situation, the boy next to him whispered, 'Say the Lord's Prayer, you fool!'*

A Period of Trial

An advertisement in *The Friend* ran, 'Student Teachers are required, willing to undergo a period of trial in Friends' Schools!'

Lindley Murray's Grammar

It is rare that a book which proved to be one of the world's best sellers was started almost casually and with so much humility. Over three-and-a-half million of Lindley Murray's Grammar were sold, and it became the standard text book of most English speaking schools of the period. Ann Tuke (afterwards Ann Alexander) and Jane Taylor (afterwards Jane Jacobs) felt their weakness in teaching grammar at the forerunner of The Mount School, so asked Lindley Murray if he would give them instruction. We have a delightful picture of them in Quaker costume, walking along the dark rough road, shod in pattens, and escorted by a man carrying a lantern. They send later a humorous, but sincere petition, which starts, 'The humble petition to the Right Hon. Lindley

---

*At this time the Friend offering prayer knelt and the rest of the Meeting stood.

Murray, teacher of the English Language.' Lindley Murray is most modest in reply, 'He fears he is not competent to write a grammar for publication!' He later consents, 'If my little labour will be confined to the schools at York and Clonmel,' and in 1795 the Grammar was published.

LINDLEY MURRAY

FRIENDS ON THEIR LAST LEGS

ILLUSTRATION FROM 'THE FRIENDS IN COUNCIL'.

CHAPTER VIII

RANDOM GLEANINGS

Friends on their Last Legs

The Darlington author*had put under the picture:
'Some of the Irish Friends had much to pass
through on their return voyage, the sea being
unusually rough, causing some in the bitterness
of their hearts to wish that the Conference had
never taken place. One Friend went so far as to
say that he did not think any good was done by
Sunday Schools. One Friend became deeply
interested in observing the movements of divers
monsters of the deep, another Friend said he
thought it was the Salmon, all agreed that
Darlington must be unhealthy to produce such
results: there were other Friends in the Cabin,
space prevents our dwelling upon them.'

Anecdotage

Friends, in kindly sending me stories, often say,
'This was told me by my mother', or, 'I wish I could
remember all the Quaker stories my father told to us,
but he never wrote them down'. It is thus evident that
many of the Friend stories we enjoy to-day were
handed down for generations round those Quaker
firesides, debarred from theatres, music, and so many
other things then called 'worldly'. I remember the
conversation in the evenings when staying with older
Friends. They were a delight which I still look back

*The Friends in Council, see page 58.

to, nearly 70 years and more, with enjoyment. I remember, when in my teens, staying with John Firth Fryer,* and on Sunday evening Alec, his son, saying to me, 'Hurry up and come to the drawing room, you'll enjoy father in his anecdotage!' The cares of the School being over, he would tell us story after story of this and that Friend, or of Quaker humorous incidents.

A Highwayman

Isabel Grubb tells in her delightful *Quaker Homespuns* a story of how an Irish Quaker girl, living in an isolated house surrounded by thick woods, heard a visiting American Friend say, when asked if they were not afraid of highwaymen, 'the angels will protect us!'

The girl puzzled over this, as she did not see how the angels would manage their wings in the thick woods. She determined to find out. So she took two candle-sticks for pistols, and dressed in her brother's clothes waylaid the two Friends as they were going away, and demanded the conventional 'money or your life'. They gave up their valuables—but no angels appeared and the 'highwayman' returned home disappointed. The coachman was so upset, that the Friends came back to the house to let him recover, and there on the dressing table they found their watches and stolen money .

This is not fiction, as Isabel Grubb's father knew the 'highwayman' in her old age, when she was the

*Headmaster of Bootham School, 1876-1899.

most beloved and revered Quaker minister in her district. The story in the book should be read in full.

Queue Stories

The young Quakeress was controlling a café queue and saw one place vacant. She said to the man at the head of the queue, 'Are you single?' She was covered with confusion by the answer, 'Yes, are you?' especially as the rest of the queue laughed.

Friend and friend

Margaret Wharton in 1941 wrote this letter to *The Friend*:

> 'As an evacuee, rather remote from *The Friend*, ordering your excellent paper was a little involved. 'Could you order *The Friend* for me?' I asked. 'Aye, *The People's Friend*.' 'No, just *The Friend*.' 'You mean, *The Girls Friend*?' 'No,' 'Does it have knitting patterns?' 'No, it is a weekly paper belonging to a religious community called Friends or Quakers'.

The assistant retired to discuss the matter with a colleague, and I overheard references to 'Peculiar People!' and the 'Salvation Army'. Returning she said, 'It's mebbe the *War Cry* yer wantin?'. I there and then delivered a short address on Quakers and Quakerism, and *The Friend* was duly ordered.

Calling the following Saturday, I eagerly asked if *The Friend* had arrived yet. 'Nae', replied the lady, 'they've gone and stopped his forty-eight hours leave!'

Railway or Washing Line

Telegram to a Friend, 'Wash out on line, cannot come'. Reply, 'Come anyway, borrow a shirt'.

Heard at The Retreat Coffee Bar

New patient, 'What are these Quakers?' Another patient—'They make oats!'

Black Beauty

I am indebted to Maurice A. Mook's article in the *Friends Intelligencer* for learning that Anna Sewell was a Quakeress, and that her *Black Beauty* is described by him as, 'the most popular Quaker book'. Several millions have been sold, and it is still selling.

Hospitality

On a Quaker 'tramp' they were assembled for allocation of hospitality. The leader astonished them by asking, 'Who would like to be slapped in a double bed?' He then read out an offer of hospitality, 'We can slap two in a double bed'.

Niagara Falls

A former farmer neighbour of Rufus Jones went to the Niagara Falls, and stood with others viewing its grandeur. A high-brow next to him exclaimed, 'Isn't it wonderful!', to which the Friend replied, 'Don't see nuthin' wonderful, what's to hinder it goin' over?'

No Hurry

A Friend in New Jersey was driving her car, and overshot the traffic lights. The 'cop' overtook her, and said, 'What's the hurry, lady?' 'No hurry', she replied, 'they will wait where I'm going'. 'And where may you be going?' said he. 'To the cemetery!' said she.

An Appendix

Frank Rowntree wrote a cheery letter to his nephew Christopher, then a boy of eleven in hospital for the removal of his appendix, in which he suggested an 'appropriate' epitaph for himself:—

'Here lies the body of F. H. Rowntree, Nephew of Drink and cousin of Poverty,*

He never stood for Council or Parliament and so remained comparatively truthful,

Above all he departed his life in full possession of his appendix,

In Death they were not separated!'

Because of the Press

John William Steel was a very busy man. He was commercial editor of the *Newcastle Chronicle*, with its morning, evening and weekly editions. Rendel Harris once said to him, with a twinkle in his eye, 'And they could not get at him because of the Press!'

Peace of Mind

Bevan Braithwaite was leaving London with a Minute for Syria and the East, when a Friend seeing him off suddenly discovered that the luggage had been put in the wrong train. In great excitement he was interviewing the Station Master and other

* His Uncle, Joseph Rowntree, had written a book on Temperance and his Cousin, B. Seebohm Rowntree, a book on Poverty.

officials, when B.B. beckoned him to his carriage and said, with his slight stutter, 'Tell Fr—Friends that I leave in great p-p-peace of mind'.

The Empty Pillion

A Quaker Minister used to ride to Meeting with his wife on a pillion behind. They carried out the injunction of preparation for Meeting so seriously that they always rode there in complete silence. He would mount gravely, then wait a sufficient time for his wife to get up, but without looking round. Then he would start off. One day he arrived, and only then discovered he had moved off before his wife had mounted, and he had left her behind.

Humour to the End

Isaac Braithwaite, the founder of Isaac Braithwaite & Sons, Kendal, was on his death bed, and the family were gathered round for the last moments. His eldest son, also Isaac, took out his watch to record the exact time of his father's demise, but whilst doing so, the old man opened his eyes, and said, 'What was the time, Isaac, that thou didst note for my passing?'

Father's Wives

Lucy Fryer, a daughter of John Firth Fryer, the then head of Bootham, had a joke, which those who were 'in the know' always enjoyed. When about twelve, she would say in a demure voice to a visitor, 'Wouldst thou like to see father's wives?' Friends knew pedigrees in those days, and a puzzled look came over their faces, as they failed to remember that John Firth Fryer had been married before, and Lucy's query seemed to suggest two previous wives: so with a furtive glance to see how her mother was taking Lucy's question, they bent eagerly over the family album, only to find they were looking at Isabella Fryer's photographs taken at different ages.

Of One Flesh

Wife,—'My dear, this ointment seems to suit me, but not thee!' Husband,—'Yes, we are of one flesh, but not of one skin'.

An Ex-Prisoner's Gift

Two maiden Friends were motoring near Maidstone, when a rough looking man flagged them down for a lift. His conversation in the car was of Maidstone Jail, and how he wanted to get as far from it as he could. The Friends got the idea that he was an escaped prisoner, and going through a town tried to carry on a whispered conversation as to whether they should drive to the police station. With her attention thus taken up, the driver ran into the back of a tram. The collision was slight, but a policeman made much of it, taking down full particulars, and saying he would certainly have to report it. The passenger was most unconcerned. After they had gone a few miles more, he asked to be put down. He thanked them for the lift, and for their friendly conversation, saying he had just finished a sentence at the jail. With a final farewell he added they would find a present under the seat. Curious to know what the present might be, they stopped the car in a mile or so, and looked. It was the policeman's note-book!

Carving the Fowl

Mary I. Manners (the authoress of *The Bishop and the Caterpillar*, *Pickled Cockles*, and other poems) and her sister used to tell how when the great surgeon Lister, who was a relative, was staying with them, they asked him to carve a chicken. Lister sat down, spent quite a time sharpening the carving knife, then gazed at the chicken for what seemed to them at least five minutes. After this he went quickly round with his carving knife, and in what seemed only a few seconds the whole chicken fell apart.

Beating Your Wife

I was speaking in Malton Market Place and the other side had put up a heckler with a tricky question, to which he demanded a plain 'yes' or 'no'. I said, 'You cannot give a plain 'yes' or 'no' to every question.' 'Oh, yes you can', he stoutly asserted. So I trotted out the old gag, 'Have you left off beating your wife? Answer 'yes', or 'no' to that!'. The heckler went as white as a sheet, and someone shouted, 'Shame'. I hastily bent down to my Chairman, Alfred Taylor, saying, 'I've put my foot into it here, what's the trouble?' Alfred said, 'He's just come out from a fortnight in prison for ill-treating his wife!' Of course there was nothing for it to prevent a row but a prompt and sincere apology, saying that the heckler was a complete stranger to me.

Cycling in Safety

In the early days of cycling, a Mount School mistress declared that 'there were two ways of preventing a cycle accident—presence of mind, or absence of body'.

The Women Patient

A popular feature of Christmas at The Retreat is the Boxing Day fancy dress dance. I was looking through some pictures by Phil May of East End life when I came across the one of a rather battered woman and two neighbours at a little distance talking. One was saying, 'What's up with Sall?' To which the other replied, 'Ain't you 'eard, she married again'.

I decided to go in this character. The matron bandaged me up and the doctor, with a few strokes of black make-up gave me a most natural black-eye. Dr. Macleod saw Arnold Rowntree approaching and hastily told me to sit amongst the women patients. Then he led Arnold up to me and introduced him to me. I shook with laughter when I heard myself addressed in his best Chairman's kindly manner towards a woman patient. Fortunately he took my hanging head and laughing as part of the patient's mental illness. Later when Arnold sat down on the edge of the platform I moved over to sit by him. He edged a little away from this flighty patient. I said something to him, and he looked round startled. Then he said, still in his best Chairman's manner, 'Would you mind saying that again'. I did, he recognised the voice, and said, 'Willie, it's never you'.

A Quaker Rowing Club

York Meeting, about 1900, had a lively set of young Friends, who formed a number of Friends' Associations, including a Rowing Club. York Women Overseers took this new club very seriously, for young women were only just beginning to free themselves from chaperone control, so that Women Overseers gravely debated if it was seemly for young men and maidens to go out in boats on the river together in the evenings, with no chaperones present. When the printed Club Rules were produced at the Women Overseers' Meeting, and carefully considered, Katherine L. Rowntree noted that young William H. Sessions, regarded by her as 'a young spark', was Captain of the Club, and that a rule said (for safety not chaperonage), 'the Captain shall see that a competent person is in charge of each boat'. She remarked icily to her fellow Overseers, 'Hum! there ought to be a rule that a competent person is in charge of the Captain'.

This leaked out, and W.H.S., although making no claims as a chaperone, felt he did understand small boats and their safety, so he chaffingly 'declared war'. This friendly 'war' was enjoyed on both sides until W.H.S. carried it further by always proposing K.L.R. for any Preparative Meeting appointment. At this, K.L.R. suggested it should cease. This was gladly agreed to, and William H. Sessions, with the joint aid of Penn's Treaty with the Indians, and some of the young men of the Meeting, drew up a formal Treaty of Peace.

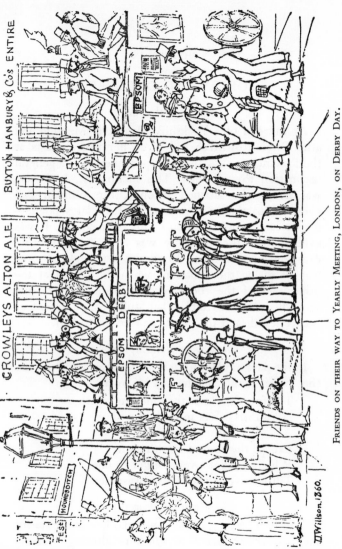

FRIENDS ON THEIR WAY TO YEARLY MEETING, LONDON, ON DERBY DAY.

CHAPTER IX

POETRY AND DOGGEREL

Poetry and the Parrot

At the end of a Yorkshire Quarterly Meeting and after Sarah Rowntree had given her many guests at the Pavement a substantial supper, there was a general inclination towards bed. This inclination, however, was not to be satisfied at once, for William Ball chose this particular moment to recite his latest poem—for he had a high opinion of his own poetry. It was evident that the company was at a stage of mild exasperation and Sarah Rowntree was seeking some way of easing the situation, when the parrot at the other end of the room, greatly inspired, suddenly screeched, 'What stuff! What stuff!' Sarah Rowntree was relieved, and the guests trotted off to bed.

Thirty Days Hath September

In the days of plain speech the Quaker could not use the above rhyme, but he had his own:

The fourth, eleventh, ninth and sixth,
Have thirty days to each affixed;
And every other thirty-one,
Except the second month alone,
Which has but twenty-eight in fine,
Till leap year gives it twenty-nine.

Nursery Rhymes

Jean E. T. Malin, of Pennsylvania, in a letter stating she had never heard of Quakers altering Nursery

Rhymes, said she would love to change, 'Rock a bye
Baby.' It was horrid, but a lovely lullaby tune.
America can, however, be said to be the cause of
the downfall of the baby, for it is supposed to have
been written by a pilgrim who went over in the
Mayflower, when he saw the Red Indians hanging
their birch-bark cradles on the boughs of trees.
Whatever we may think of it now, the rhyme is
said to be the first poem produced on American soil
by the white people.

Merrily Danced the Quaker's Wife

There have been various endeavours to trace this
curious poem and one of the best is that contained in
the *Friends Quarterly* for January 1948. It was evidently
set to a tune for the blind fiddler played it in Scott's
Redgauntlet. It would appear that the tune was better
than the rhyme, for Scott calls it 'a well-known and
popular measure', but refers to the words as 'the
insulting air'.

The article in the *Friends Quarterly* by Alec S.
Fryer suggests its source as an obscure comic opera
of the early eighteenth century, and gives a Scottish
version

The Quaker's Wife

The Quaker's wife sat doon to bake
Wi' a' her bairns aboot her;
She baked them every ane a cake,
An' the miller he wants his mouter.
Sugar an' spice an' a' things nice,
An' a' things vera guid in it:

An' then the Quaker sat doon to play
A tune upon her spinet.
Merrily danced the Quaker's wife,
An' merrily danced the Quaker;
Merrily danced the Quaker's wife
An' merrily danced the Quaker.

There is a version that 'The Quaker's Wife *got up* to bake', which is more likely. Another version reads, 'And merrily danced the Quakers', plural of Quaker.

This, the Opies* say was taken from an Edinburgh manuscript of 1770-80.

What were the Overseers of their Meeting doing not to stop such 'goings on'—dancing, owning a spinet, and playing on it ! ! !

In my first volume I related how German girls were convinced that Quakers danced in their religious services. I wonder if the same belief in Scotland gave rise to the words of 'Merrily Danced the Quaker's Wife'. It is, however, well authenticated, and it appeared in Oswald's *Pocket Companion for the Guitar* printed about 1755, and it was a favourite of Burns.

Punch published in 1852 a satire on the Quakers, inspired by at least some of them refusing to shut their shops on the day of the Duke of Wellington's funeral, which started with this rhyme.

'*Vagaries Under Broad-Brims*'
Merrily danced the Quaker's wife,
And Merrily danced the Quaker;

*See page 90.

She had been a preacher all her life,
And her spouse an undertaker.
He made it his special pride and boast
At war to be a railer,
And couldn't tell which he hated most,
A soldier or a sailor.

Not that old Broadbrim bore ill will,
Or was actually malicious,
But anything that retrench'd his bill,
He held inexcusably vicious,
He called it the act of ruffian brutes,
To die on the field of battle,
And pay no more for pall and mutes
Than so many slaughter'd cattle.

Yet he gave a new half-crown one day
To Steggars, the tall policeman,
And said, 'Thou worthily earns't thy pay
In guarding my home and peace, man.'
A Quaker's saving instinct's strong,
Like a snipe's, that lives by suction;
But the bird, it seems, has a head as long
At drawing a clear deduction.

And thus they all are freakish elves,
Doing things out of season,
For which no mortal but themselves
Can ever assign a reason.
On the burial day of our glorious chief
They open'd their shops in Gloucester,
And declared in print for their mind's relief,
The good old duke an imposter.

They are harmless neighbours, on the whole,
Though rather close and selfish,
And have, I believe, a responsible soul,
Which isn't the case with shellfish.
But it hurts their creed and pride to pay
Any regular Gospel teachers:
And St. Paul would be 'struck all-a-heap' with
dismay,
If he heard their female preachers.

A Quaker baby never was seen,
Or a Quaker boy a-playing;
They never are born till turn'd eighteen,
And whether they suck, there's no saying.
A Ranter can sow, a Baptist mow,
A Romanist build your dwelling,
But the Quaker's forte, as all men know,
Is the knack of buying and selling.

Friend Fry hath a deal of active zeal
As a Peace Society talker.
But I'd rather consult, on the common weal,
Our old friend, Hookey Walker.
The man who fights for his country's rights
He would coolly dub an unholy one
And freely adjure, to make trade secure,
Victoria for Napoleon.

Sure they are the most eccentric race,
That ever was born of Adam;
They would wear their hats to Her Majesty's face,
And refuse her the title of Madam.

But the world has room for every one,
And they don't require compassion;
So long may they live to enjoy their fun
In their own remarkable fashion.

The poem is not too unkindly, as the last four lines show. To-day we should think the Quakers rather 'asked for it', for *The Friend* published an editorial on the death of the Duke of Wellington, in which it went so far as to cast doubts on a place in heaven for the national hero.

Dance and Sing

It was Tom Twistleton, a West Riding Dialect poet, who described a view as so beautiful that:—

'Such scenes as these, when seen in spring
Would mak' a Quaker dance and sing
An' mak' a clown turn poet.'

Lines on a Quakeress' Birthday

Again returns my natal day,
With many mercies blest,
And He who placed the structure here
Will prop it up another year,
If He should think it best.

Next I will quote a poem from the second edition of
*Friends in Council**

The Charge of the Drab Brigade

Broad brimmed their helmets were,
Linen was marked with care,
Collarless coats they wear,
Noble Eight Hundred.
Matrons and maidens there
Some dark and others fair,
Caps worn to keep back hair
Somewhat in subjection. . . .

Sessional Committees too
Guarded this chosen crew,
Apprehending that some few
Might frequent taverns.
Their's not to reason why,
Useless it were to fly,
From the keen piercing eye
Of the Committee. . . .

Committees to right of them,
Committees to left of them
Committees behind them,
Friends' houses thundered
Elm Ridge took ninety-two.
And Pierremont not a few
Into Beechwood they flew
Till the world wondered. . . .

With milk and honey blest,
And in fine linen dressed,

*See page 58.

Friends always have the best
Of this world's faring
Carriages at command,
Servants a goodly band
Footstools on every hand,
Thus the Cross bearing. . . .

Maytime

Quarterly Meeting is held at St. Austell, in Cornwall, in the hay season, which is usually wet, so the farmers have a rhyme:—

'Now varmer, now varmer,
Tak' care ou your hye,
For 'tis the Quakkers' great mittin to-dye'

Whilst the lads call after the Friend children:—

Lord av masey 'pon us,
Keep the Quakkers from us'.

Lettsom

John Lettsom was a learned Quaker physician of the latter half of the eighteenth century. He is said to have had the largest practice in London. Someone who did not quite appreciate his great knowledge composed the following rhyme:—

When any sick to me apply
    I physics, bleeds and sweats 'em,
If, after that, they choose to die,
    What's that to me? I Lettsom.

Slow Coaches

On a Committee to revise the *Book of Discipline*, Josiah Tottenham worked more speedily than the rest of the Committee, which caused William Ball to put round this rhyme. The version in *The Friend* is:—

> Slow coaches all are we,
>   Besides Josiah's carriage.
> Four hours we've spent on 'love',
>   He's ready now for 'marriage'.

Edward Grubb, however, sent me this:—

> Slow coaches are we all, compared
>   With dear Josiah's carriage.
> Two hours in Love, and now prepared
>   To enter into Marriage.

Post No Bills

The Alexanders and Hills were well-known Quaker families in Limerick 150 years ago and had shops opposite to one another. Joshua Hill, from his autocratic, commanding manner, won for himself the nickname of 'The Great Commander.' A bill poster posted a bill on his premises, which displeased him mightily, and resulted in the following verse:—

> Post no bills on Joshua Hills
> For he's the Great Commander,
> But post them on the opposite side,
> On Snuffy Alexander.

Sporting with a Brick

Bootham School long years ago had a parody of Robert Southey's *Battle of Blenheim* about James Edmund Clark. I can only remember the first six lines:—

> It was a summer's evening,
> James Edmund's work was done,
> And he before the Bootham door
> Was sitting in the sun;
> Beside him sporting with a brick
> His little sonny Roderick.

Poetry in a Latin Lesson

A. Neave Brayshaw on occasion introduced poems into his Bootham latin lessons, such as this which differentiates between two similar words:—

> Os Ossis, a bone, is a curious word,
> Ossium is the genitive case,
> The rest is quite regular as you will see.
> Os Oris, a mouth or a face.

Friends House, May 1946

The war days when soap was rationed to a very meagre amount is recalled by these verses by an unknown hand.

> Time was when soap and I were well acquainted,
> Time was when it came ready to my hand,
> Friends House could show no finger-tips less tainted,
> None cleaner washed than I in all the land.

Then came a time of scarcity—nay famine—
The void containers mocked our fondest hope,
'Twere better not too closely to examine
How one could wash in water wanting soap.

Now in the joyful week of Yearly Meeting
Some godly mind to cleanliness is stirred,
To me it brings occasion for completing
My toilet with that soap so long deferred.

Moral: Soap deferred maketh the dirt stick.

World Conference

The walrus and the carpenter,
They missed their sand and breakers,
But smiled like anything to see
Such quantities of Quakers.
'They look to be', the walrus said,
'God fearing money makers'.

George Fox

George Fox, whose portrait here you see,
Believed in great simplicity,
He wore a homespun coat of grey
And leathern breeches, so they say.
His Yes and No were plain and flat,
To kings he would not doff his hat.

'There is an Inner Light,' he cried,
'Which every child of God can guide.
Such will from oaths and fightings cease,
And tread the happy paths of peace,
To wealth and rank no heed will pay
But treat all persons the same way.'

In silence in their meeting-place
These heard God's voice and sought his grace.
In ways of quiet friendliness
They sought to heal and help and bless.
And those whose still pursue these ends
Are called THE SOCIETY OF FRIENDS.'

Reprinted by permission, from *A Rhyme Book of Christian Men*
by Vera Walker, (S.C.M. Press.)

R. B. Seebohm sent me a poem, each verse about a
Quaker worthy of the time. I will give two of the
verses. The poem was printed, price 6d., and ran to
a second edition. It is entitled:

Quakerieties for 1838

James Backhouse, James Backhouse,
Dissensions still rack us,
And many their birthright have sold;
Yet we count it no loss,
To get rid of the dross,
While we keep all the purified gold!
                              James Backhouse,
While we keep all the purified gold!

Betsy Fry, Betsy Fry,
Where the fatherless lie,
And the widow, we find thee: 'tis there!
In the prison-house cell,
That the soft accents dwell;
And the culprit exults in thy prayer!
                              Betsy Fry,
And the culprit exults in thy prayer!

The weddings at close intervals of five Quakeresses of Hitchin about 1857 resulted in a poem of 14 verses, by Lawson Thompson. I give but one verse and the rejoinder.

A Lay after Lord Macaulay

The harvest of the lawcourts
    This year must others reap
Unsettled till another term
    Must doubtful causes keep
Or some one of his legal friends
    His client fees must share
For Seebohmius the Barrister
    Has gone to court elsewhere.

Frederick Seebohm replied in one verse, as follows:

Thomsonius legis filius,
    A luckless wight was he,
And peradventure envious
    Of those who victors be.
He joined not in the conquest
    And so no laurels won,
But he could not lull his soul to rest
    When he saw the deed was done.
Like the Roman bard he gravely sped
    At first, but alas ere long
Throwing away his shield he fled
    Ah me! and wrote a song.

A Neave Brayshaw's recitations were very popular with the boys of Bootham School and of a wide Quaker circle. So much so that a private gramophone recording was made in 1935 which many Friends will still recall with gratitude and delight. The following three poems are transcribed from one of these records.

THE SLIDE
An Exercise in Strong Verbs

The Butcher's boy had made a slide in the middle of
the road;
It was the very longest slide that ever mortal sload.
The Baker's boy espied it and observed: 'Now this is
good,
I'll have a go at that there slide' and subsequently
slood.

The Village Patriach upon the slippery surface trod,
Most inadvertently and unintentionally he slod.
Then Mrs. Smith of middle age, her youthful past
rewened,
Glanced round, saw no one coming and started off and
slewed.

The Curate passing down the Street, remembered that
he had
Some skill in sliding as a boy and elegantly slad.
The Doctor followed bravely with a cry of: 'Who's
afraid',
And suffered much from somersault, in agony he slaid.
The Constable remarked: 'Well', he said 'I never did,
I shall be sliding next myself,' which, having said, he
slid.

At the end of the slide they all came down on a heap of
frozen mud,
And sat there and were sorry that they had ever slud.
And did not love the boy who made, in the middle of
the road,
The Slide that was the longest slide that ever mortal
sload.

THE EOHIPPUS

(*The Eohippus was the geological ancestor of the horse.*)

There was once a little animal, no bigger than a fox
And on five toes he scampered over tertiary rocks.
They called him Eohippus and they called him very
small
And they thought him of no value when they thought
of him at all.
For the lumpish old Dinoceras and Cheiropteran so
slow.
Were the heavy aristocracy in days of long ago.

Said the little Eohippus 'I'm going to be a horse
And on my middle finger nail shall run my earthly
course.
I'm going to have a flowing tail, I'm going to have a
mane,
I'm going to stand fourteen hands high on the
psychozoic plain.'

The Cheiropteran was horrified, the Dinoceras was
shocked
And they chased the Eohippus but he skipped away
and mocked.

Then they laughed enormous laughter, and they
                              groaned enormous groans
And they bade young Eohippus go view his father's
                                              bones.

Quoth they 'You always were as small and mean as
                                          now we see
And that's conclusive evidence you're always going
                                             to be'.
'What, be a great tall handsome beast with hooves to
                                         gallop on
Why you'd have to change your nature' said the
                              Loxia Lophiedon.
They considered him disposed of and retired with
                                     gait serene,
For that was the way they argued in the early eocene.

There was an anthropoidal ape far smarter than the
                                             rest.
And everything that they could do he always did the
                                             best.
So they naturally disliked him and they gave him
                                   shoulders cool
And when they had to mention him they said he was a
                                            fool.

Cried this pretentious ape one day 'I'm going to be a
                                              man
And stand upright and hunt and fight, and conquer all I
                                             can

I'm going to cut down forest trees, to make the houses
higher
I'm going to kill the Mastodon, I'm going to make a
fire'.

Loud screamed the anthropoidal apes with laughter
wild and gay
And they tried to catch that boastful one but he always
got away.
Then they yelled at him in chorus which he didn't
mind a bit
And they pelted him with coconuts which didn't
seem to hit.
And then they brought him arguments which they
thought of much avail
To prove that this preposterous attempt was sure to
fail.

Said the sages 'In the first place the thing cannot be
done,
In the second, if it could be, there would not be any
fun
And the third and most conclusive, and admitting no
reply
You would have to change your nature: we should like
to see you try'.
And then they yelled in chorus those lean and hairy
shapes
For these things passed as arguments—with the
Anthropoidal apes.

There was a neolithic man, an enterprising wight,

Who kept his chopping implements unusually bright,

Unusually clever he, unusually brave,

And he drew delightful mammoths on the borders of
his cave.

To his neolothic neighbours who were startled and
surprised
He said 'My friends in course of time we shall be
civilised.
We're going to live in cities, we're going to fight in
wars,
We're going to eat three times a day without the
natural cause
We're going to turn life upside down about a thing
called gold
We're going to want the earth and take as much as we
can hold
We're going to wear great piles of stuff, outside our
proper skins
We're going to have diseases and accomplishments and
sins.'

Then they all rose up in fury against their boastful
friend
For prehistoric patience cometh quickly to an end.
Cried one 'This is tyrannical, utopian, absurd'
Said another 'What a stupid life, too dull upon my
word'.

Cried all, 'These things can never come, you idiotic
child,
You can't change human nature', and they all sat
back and smiled.
Thought they an answer to this last it will be hard to
find.
It was a clinching argument to the neolithic mind.

DIVES AND LAZARUS

Did you ever hear of Dives who lived in Palestine,
A marvellous rich man was he and clothed in super-
fine.
His table groaned with loads of food, his wine by gallons
ran,
No wonder he grew sleek and stout, just like an
Alderman.

Another man named Lazarus, homeless and sick and
poor,
In hope to beg the rich man's crumbs, lay at the rich
man's door
He heard the sound of mirth within, but not a friend
had he,
Except the dogs who licked his sores in silent
sympathy.

You'd think it strange that such a thing should happen
here below
But that was in a far off land, a long while ago.

Now Dives daily feasted, and was gorgeously arrayed,
Not at all because he liked it, but because t'was good
for trade.
That the people might have calico he clothed himself
in silk,
And surfeited himself on cream, that they might get
their milk.

He fed five hundred servants that the poor might not
lack bread,
And had his vessels made of gold that they might get
the lead.
And ee'n to show his sympathy with the deserving
poor,
He did no useful work at all, that they might do the
more.

You'll think it very very strange but then, of course,
you know
'Twas in a far off country and a long while ago.

Poor Lazarus at length became too weak with death to
strive,
He was evidently not one of the fittest to survive,
So on one frosty night about a quarter to eleven,
He looked up at the silent stars, then died and went to
heaven.

Now Dives too was waxing old, and presently fell ill.
Whereon a lawyer was called in to make a mighty will.

And when Dives' sons and daughters came to hear his
last farewell,
He bade them follow in his steps, then died and
went to hell.

I don't think God would venture now to treat a rich
man so,
But this was such a long way off and so very long ago.

Farewell

I can only hope that you, dear reader, will in your charity, declare this book 'full of right wittie conceits'.

I trust none of my stories will shock any reader; if one does, please remember I live at York. A story we tell against ourselves is that when James I came to England he found the London shoemakers could not make shoes good enough for his Scottish troops, so he sent a messenger riding to Edinburgh, for 10,000 brogues. The man arrived drunk and said, 10,000 rogues. Much surprised they emptied the jails and sent the men marching South under guard. James heard of this, and hastily sent to stop them. The messengers stopped the rogues at York—and there they have remained ever since!

LAUGHTER IN QUAKER GREY

by W. H. SESSIONS

The general reader will discover in this first volume of Quaker stories much that is of amusement and interest, especially concerning the old Quaker ways and costume.

Friends themselves will also enjoy reading in these stories some of the almost forgotten incidents in the history of the Society and will appreciate the humour of the Quaker rhymes.

THE FRIENDS MEETING HOUSE

by HUBERT LIDBETTER

This book with its wealth of architectural and historical detail concerning Friends Meeting Houses is the result of many years of research and collection by a well-known Quaker architect. Its pages contain many photographs and line drawings which the text inter-relates with great effect and as Professor Sir Albert Richardson so aptly says in his Foreword, the author has thus provided a silver key to their character and dignity.

OTHER QUAKER PUBLICATIONS

Available From

SESSIONS OF YORK

LAUGHTER IN QUAKER GREY by William H. Sessions. The first volume of humorous Quaker anecdotes revealing Quaker character and foibles

TRAVELLERS JOY by Hannah Taylor and Ruthanna Hadley. Recipes, Meal Patterns, and Quaker hospitality around the world, including tables in U.K., American and European measures

THE TUKES OF YORK by W. K. & E .M. Sessions. Narrative of the well-known York Quaker family. Published in association with Friends Home Service Committee

ROGER CLARK'S anthology of pieces written for the Village Essay Society of Street, Somerset—selected by Percy A. Lovell

QUAKER ENCOUNTERS : Vol. 1 Friends and Relief, by John Ormerod Greenwood: the first comprehensive study of the history of British Quaker Relief work from the Napoleonic Wars to 1945

OUR QUAKER HERITAGE, collected and edited by Kenneth H. Southall: photographs and word pictures of early Quaker Meeting Houses built prior to 1720 and in use to-day. Published in association with Friends Home Service Committee

THE FRIENDS MEETING HOUSE by Hubert Lidbetter, FRIBA. Historical Survey of Friends' places of Worship from the beginning of Quakerism including plans and photographs

THE BEGINNINGS OF QUAKERISM by Wm. C. Braithwaite: the 1970 Cambridge University Press publication now distributed by Sessions of York

THE SECOND PERIOD OF QUAKERISM by Wm. C. Braithwaite: the 1961 Cambridge University Press Publication now distributed by Sessions of York